With Love

365 days of heartfelt wisdom

To Neelam
With Love
Tim x

Tim Brister

GOWOR
INTERNATIONAL PUBLISHING

Personal Note From The Publisher

Hi there!

As the Founder of Gowor International Publishing, I make it part of my practice to offer a personal review for my authors about their book. The reason I do this is so that you, the reader, can glean a further understanding into why this book is about to become a valuable part of your life.

From all of my experiences so far, I can safely say that Tim is by far one of the most beautiful men I have encountered in my life (and I mean beautiful in the spiritual sense). The level of love that I have felt while interacting with this strong and loving man has had a healing impact on me in the deepest of ways: and now you are about to be impacted, too.

With Love shares profound daily wisdom about life with its readers, written straight from Tim's heart to yours. This book will gift you with the perfect message that you need in the moment you, no doubt, need it the most. It will journey with you throughout your year as you keep it on your bedside table or office desk, inspiring you to the core — one message, one day at a time. I know that you will be touched by Tim's heart in *With Love* the same way that I have been touched by his words and his extraordinary presence.

May you thoroughly enjoy the next 365 days of your life... for they will be better for having read this book!

With inspiration,

Emily Gowor
Founder of Gowor International Publishing

Acknowledgements

The gratitude and love I feel for all those who have contributed to the creation of *With Love* knows no bounds. To all my friends who took the time to read, like and comment on my posts on Facebook — those comments were the catalyst for *With Love*.

There are many people who have in some way contributed to major shifts, including Garry Welsh, Victor Marino, Tony Robbins, Joseph McClendon III, Neale Donald Walsch, Deepak Chopra, and Animas Centre For Coaching. Thank you all.

Finally, thank you to my family, and in particular, the three people who transformed my life in very different ways. Thank you to Louise, Jack and Harry; without your unconditional love, none of this would have been possible. For believing in me and loving me even when I was short of belief and love for myself: Thank you.

This book is dedicated to all those who have loved, mentored, nurtured and inspired me. Thank you, I love you all.

A special word for the unconditional love of Louise, my soul mate and wife. You are the greatest gift of my life. Thank you.

Introduction

Have you ever had one of those days?

When life just feels like it's harder than it ought to be.

And then, whilst scrolling through social media you come across a few words that really hit the mark, words that somehow get straight to your heart.

This book is for everyone who has ever had one of those days. Even if you don't have those days anymore, this book is still for you. The words in this book are written from my heart to connect with your heart, to enable you to amplify the connection that you have with your heart.

There are 365 entries. Every day of the year you could read a page a day, from 1 through to 365. Or perhaps let your intuition guide you to read whichever page calls to you in that moment. Or you could read the whole book from cover to cover in a matter of hours. There are no rules, this book is for you, enjoy it in the way which serves you best.

Wishing you a life abundant in loving moments.

With love

Tim Brister

1

*B*eing present...

Sometimes being present can feel like the big, difficult thing that we need to do, but nothing could be further from the truth.

We can experience being present whilst

out running,

meditating,

waiting for the kettle to boil.

Being present is something we are BEING whilst DOING any number of day-to-day activities. We can be present for a few moments or a few minutes or longer; it really doesn't matter how long. The important thing for us all is to experience being present to recharge and reconnect.

Be present for a moment or two or three or more today.

With love

x

2

*T*rust your instincts. Trust your feelings...

If something doesn't feel right, then stop!

Giving yourself the gift of time and space to acknowledge and to truly listen to your instincts not only supports your spiritual well-being, but in addition, you will often stop getting involved in something that doesn't serve you... Win-win.

And if after the period of reflection you feel that it's right to continue being involved, then you can do that with greater certainty than before... Win-win.

Or to put it another way: Trust yourself first, then you will be able to trust others.

With love

x

*F*ollow your heart. Our minds are amazing and are essential to our survival but our hearts truly know our inner purpose and journey.

With love

x

*I*n this fast paced, outcome oriented, fail/succeed, pass/fail, win/lose world that we inhabit it's easy to let our ego take control to protect us from the "dangers" we fear.

Be aware that those fears are self created and sustained by the ego because the ego fears losing control, it fears our creativity and most of all it fears death.

That doesn't feel like a free, creative and heart-filled place to be.

Today, listen to the fears that come up and gently question where they came from and really, I mean really, are they real or creations of the ego?

With love

x

5

*B*eing grateful, living with gratitude is truly life transforming.

There's something magical that happens in our lives when we start to be grateful for all the wonders in our life, no matter how small or commonplace. For example, the air that we breath, the beating or our heart, the beauty of nature, etc., etc.

Make today a day of being grateful, take time to stop and notice everything around you and everything in your life you are grateful for. Appreciate that moment and every moment.

With love

x

6

*T*here seems to be a paradox in living in abundance, without scarcity or lack whilst living in the moment, making the most of every single precious moment.

Surely, knowing that there is abundance, and therefore an abundance of moments, could lead us to let some moments pass without being present and making the most of that moment. After all there's another moment coming right up, and another and then another.

What I've observed is that when we are truly being grateful, being abundant and being present, then we are making the most of every moment.

Perhaps, rather than looking at the moments and thinking how to make the most of them... instead, be present, be grateful and be abundant. Then you'll be making the most of every moment — always.

With love

x

7

*L*ive each day with a sparkle, with love, having fun.

It's so easy to conform with the unwritten (and some written) rules of our developed societies. Sadly, there's usually not a whole lot of sparkle, love and fun evident during many of our day-to-day activities.

As children we all knew how to have fun, to sparkle/be mischievous, and we all knew that we are loved and we are lovable.

Make sure that today your day sparkles with fun and love. Notice how that feels... You'll probably want to sparkle some more tomorrow...

With love

x

8

*W*e hear our political and spiritual leaders talk of world peace and no doubt their words are heartfelt.

However, like many feelings, many outcomes, peace in the world begins with every one of us individually being at peace with ourselves.

How can we expect the world to be peaceful if every day many of us are battling with ourselves in an inner war/ struggle that diminishes our beauty and leads to conflict within?

Today, pause for a moment, breath slowly and deeply. In that moment feel the inner calm that brings us closer to being at peace with ourselves.

Have a beautiful, peaceful day.

With love

x

*R*emember that you have it within you to make your life a masterpiece.

Don't wait for a special day, or time, or event to "be yourself" or to feel good about your life. The label we attach to any time period or event does not determine how you feel... That's down to YOU!

Make the choice to feel outstanding every moment of every day. Let your life be a masterpiece, let your life be a life that you are proud of.

With love

x

10

A question: Why do we search outside ourselves for that which we truly want when everything we need is within us?

Our human mind might want toys, houses, partners, children, etc., etc., and there's nothing wrong with any of those things BUT none of those are what our soul is here for.

Our soul is here for love, our soul is here for us to remember to be love because we are love.

With love

x

11

*I*nner peace, calm and serenity...

With a sense of inner peace, calm and serenity we feel grounded.

When we feel ground, the events and experiences in our lives are less likely to disturb our being and our knowing about who we are.

Relish every moment of your life, and when events disturb you, breathe, be quiet (inside and out) and notice whatever comes to you in that moment.

And when I say relish every moment... have a BLAST!

With love

x

12

*O*ur planet is overrun with and run by fearful people. Don't let this conditioned fear diminish your beauty, your love and your dreams. Your heart knows the truth. Let your heart shape your life.

With love

x

13

*T*oday, play like a child. Just for a few moments (or longer if you're enjoying it).

Let your heart sing and your spirit celebrate the freedom and fun of your human existence.

With love

x

14

*T*he flow of magnificence that blesses us all is one of the great gifts of human existence. We are born in the flow and we live in that flow until slowly, slowly our flow is blocked by "life", usually disguised as well-intentioned, caring friends and relatives who want to protect us.

The truth is, we don't need protecting, we belong in the flow of magnificence because it's from there that our greatness will shine through and from there we reveal the brilliant shining light at the centre of our being.

With love

x

15

*L*iving a life without joy is not living: it's more like an existence. Yet for many of us we are present with joy only for infrequent, fleeting moments.

Remember how being joyful feels for you, remember those times when you felt complete joy. Now, with those memories fresh in your mind go create some joy right now.

Please remember that how and what we choose to be and feel in any given moment is entirely our choice. Today choose joy and notice how you feel and how others interact with you because (and here's the kicker) joy tends to spread.

EnJOY.

With love

x

16

*W*aking up — something we do every day of our human existence.

But are we really awake or living in a sleeping trance? What do I mean by that?

Ask how connected you are to nature, to your soul, your heart, to love, to those who love you, to the truth of who you are.

When we are truly awake there is a feeling, a sense of connection that is just beautiful.

This might feel like a test or a challenge, but it really isn't. Life is for us all to enjoy. Just notice and enjoy the moments of connection and awakening in every day.

With love

x

17

*B*eing grateful sounds simple, though it's not always easy. As we are presented with challenges in our human existence, it's often too easy to respond and react from an ungrateful place.

We might not even notice until much later (if we notice at all), but the universe notices. The universe notices when we are being grateful and when we are not.

One of the magical aspects of the universe is that mysteriously we get more of what we're being. So when we're consistently being grateful we notice more and more to be grateful for. Conversely, when we're not being grateful, we feel dissatisfied and out of alignment with our soul.

Choose to be grateful and notice how much more gratitude there is in your life. Trust the universe to provide... First though, you need to take the leap and be grateful every moment of every day. Then miracles will occur.

With love

x

18

A short, powerful message:

Remember to love, because love is all there is.

No matter how old you are, what stage your life is at, how hopeless things might feel, please don't wait a single day; be love and live from a place of love today and every day, because... well, just because it's the only thing that matters. It really is.

With love

x

19

Be true to yourself, trust your inner compass, listen to your heart, and you will discover true contentment.

There are times when we observe people acting in a way that does not lead to contentment. It might feel uncomfortable to us because we sense the misalignment but for them it is far worse; they are compromising the joy in their lives.

Each and every one of us is an integrated being. Therefore, misalignment in one aspect of our lives leads to misalignment and discontent in other areas of our lives.

Every moment, act with integrity, follow your heart, and magically the joy of contentment will manifest for you.

With love

x

20

*I*magine that you could look at any problems/challenges in a different way, in a way that enabled you to realise that they really are gifts to be played with and enjoyed.

Remember a time when you were a child and it was wet, wet, wet. There are puddles everywhere. As a child, what do puddles mean? They mean fun, they are to be played in, jumped in, splashed in. Puddles are gifts to be enjoyed.

How do you view puddles as an adult?

Today, take one of these problems/challenges and view it as a puddle through the eyes and mind of the child that plays in puddles. Treat these problems/challenges as gifts to be played with. Jump in with both feet.

Maybe you'll have a more playful day as a result.

With love

X

21

*F*rom my heart to yours - enjoy the most beautiful, love-filled, connected day.

Always remember that you are the creator of your own experience and that along with everyone else we are co-creators of our collective experience.

Let's create some awesome experiences today.

With love

x

22

*C*hange...

Strange thing change. It usually feels uncomfortable, sometimes challenging, but always different (otherwise it wouldn't be change!).

Embrace change with all your heart and soul, for it is through change that we continue to grow. Remembering that we are subject to the laws of nature, which means that we're either growing or dying.

Practice change every day, travel a different route, resequence your daily routine, wear your watch on the opposite wrist, remove your watch completely! Do anything, but do something different every day. Get used to the small changes and magically the big changes don't feel quite so big.

With love

x

23

*W*e are all, at our hearts, creative, loving beings with an abundance of gifts to share.

Somewhere along the way, we humans have suppressed/sidelined/silenced the creativity and love we have to share.

It feels to me that right now, more than ever, what the world needs is for loving creativity to become more prominent. We can only make that happen one person at a time, starting with ourselves.

Today, notice your loving and creative feelings. Enjoy and dwell in those feelings. Find a way, however small, to share your creativity and love... Step by step, one by one we will enhance the experience we share.

With love

x

24

*O*ur lives can get so cluttered with stuff: objects, people, events, jobs, etc. — so much stuff that can feel important and sometimes threatening, but really what is important?

There is beauty all around us, there are miracles unfolding every second of every day. Most important of all is love. Love is all there is.

There is nothing wrong with or bad about stuff. Please remember that the context for life is love.

First and foremost be love, appreciate the beauty and miracles we are blessed to experience every day, and have a blast!

With love

x

25

*F*rom my heart to yours, enjoy a beautiful day — a day abundant in love, abundant in sparkles, abundant in passion, abundant in health, abundant in connection and abundant in laughter.

It's no less than you deserve today and every day.

With love

x

26

*B*e yourself, follow your heart, be true to yourself... All great sentiments, but what does it mean to truly be you?

The key to being you is that it is a "being" and not a "doing". Being you comes from inside, through honouring you and trusting you to have all the answers. And when you don't believe you have the answer, then trust whatever is coming up for you.

There's no doubt that we can "do" things that open up our inner flow of energy for us to "be" our true selves. We can meditate, we can breathe deeply, we can acquire knowledge on how to live a more fulfilling life, etc., etc.

But whilst some doing does contribute towards the being, it is the being that enables our true self to flow. And if there is one "doing" above all others that will move you closer to your true self it is to...

Listen to your heart.

With love

x

27

*L*ook around as you go about your daily life and what do you see, hear and feel? ...

Silence

Disconnection

Misery

Pain

Everyone... It doesn't have to be this way! Wake up and decide to enjoy this time on this planet. It really is a choice we all have. Granted, the world tends to be set up to view misery, pain, disconnection and disease as the norm. But it really doesn't have to be this way.

From my heart.

With love

x

28

*B*e the love that you want to see and feel in the world.

Today, be loving towards everyone and everything. Every person you interact with, however briefly, send them love. Be loving towards every miracle of nature, the beautiful green leaves on the trees, the refreshing rain that is essential to survival of life on earth, even the midges that might have bitten you... be loving to everything.

Notice how you feel as you're being loving. Also notice how those around you interact with you as you're being loving.

Maybe, just maybe, you'll decide to be loving tomorrow as well.

With love

x

29

*R*esistance is a sign of misalignment. Beware and be aware.

Whether you feel resistance in your heart, your mind or your body, please, please, please LISTEN! There is something that's not as your soul wants it to be. Don't mask the resistance. Most of us use food, alcohol, nicotine, drugs, exercise to distract us from the messages we really need to receive.

Next time you feel some discomfort or resistance, notice your reflex reaction, then pause, listen to your soul's message. What could be the purpose of the resistance? How does repeating your reflex patterns of behaviour and responses enable the underlying message to be heard (or not be heard)? Then choose your response and notice how that feels for you.

With love

x

30

*V*iew each day as a magical adventure, just as you did as a child, when everything was a playground, an opportunity to explore, push boundaries, try something new.

Today it's commonplace for people to function day to day on autopilot: Get up at the same time, prepare for work in the same way, travel to work on the same route, endure 8+ hours at work, travel the same route home, eat, do stuff, sleep and repeat...

Where has all that adventure and magic gone? All the magic and adventure that we experienced as children?

The answer is that it's still there.

We have it within us to experience magic and adventure every second of every day.

We can be adventurous whenever we want to, we can do different things every day.

Do we need to get up at the same time every day, or could we perhaps get up earlier and meditate or read or sit in silent reflection?

Could we travel a different route to work?

Could we enjoy instead of endure our workday?

After work could we do something different, e.g., go for a walk, chat with our family, connect with old friends, etc.?

Just making some small changes, doing just one or two different things every day will rekindle magic and adventure. Remember that we all want magic and adventure in our lives, but somehow we seem to forget that as we move from childhood into adulthood.

Today, be adventurous, surprise someone, live magically and enjoy the life and energy that you bring to the world.

With love

x

31

*I*f today is one of "those" days — whatever that means for you — then be loving of yourself first and foremost. That's not a self-centred thing to do, it's an essential thing to do, because if we don't love ourselves, what makes us believe we can truly love others?

Love is all there is.

With love

x

*S*how love, show compassion and care.

Everyone is on their journey, most people feeling more pain than pleasure and many just struggling to make it through the day/week/month/year/life.

If we first of all connect with ourselves, our own soul, that is a beautiful, fulfilling experience. Then, from that place of personal connection we are available to connect fully with others.

Many people simply want to be heard, to feel that someone cares. When we truly connect with someone — and that someone can be a long-time friend, acquaintance or a complete stranger — it is magical, it raises the vibration of both us and them and therefore the planet... As I said, magical.

Today, be fully connected with yourself, notice how that feels, then connect with others in a caring, loving way — even if only for a brief few seconds — and notice how magical that feels.

Caring and compassion.

With love

x

33

*H*ave you noticed how few people actually look where they're going. I don't even mean at a life direction level, I mean just going about their day-to-day lives.

If you haven't noticed, then take a look today as you're out and about. It's quite staggering.

What causes people to avoid looking where they are going? If we asked ten people we'd get at least five different answers, such as looking in shop windows, reading a paper, being on the phone, surfing the net, browsing Facebook, chatting with friends, etc., and we've all seen people doing these things. We might have even caught ourselves doing them.

What about if all those things weren't causes but were merely symptoms? What if the underlying cause was unconscious disconnection? By disconnecting from the present, people can avoid looking at where they are going.

But what if disconnection could itself be a symptom of fear? Fear is the driver of most people's state of being, and from a place of fear we cannot be connected with ourselves or anyone else.

We are born fearless. Fear is something we learn as we go through life. But as with anything, it's a choice. We can choose in every moment whether we want to be fearful or be connected and loving or any number of states of being.

Something to think about.

With love

x

34

*B*eing grateful has been transformational for me and being grateful continues to transform my life.

Take some moments today to be present and grateful for this moment, for the miracles that are taking place in this moment. The miracles of nature, the miracles created by humankind, the miracles of life.

There is so much to be grateful for in every moment of every day.

With love

x

35

Challenges appear in our lives at exactly the right time to enable us to remember what we need to remember in that moment.

Yet it almost never feels that way in that moment. But if it did feel comfortable then it wouldn't be much of a challenge!

Embrace the challenges in your life. Recognise every challenge as an opportunity to grow.

Most of all, when challenges come up, search within yourself for the lesson, for the growth. Whilst challenges often appear to be externally triggered/caused, the growth, the remembering, the lessons are within you. Searching externally for the lessons is futile and only results in similar challenges being repeated until the growth within you takes place and the lessons are remembered.

Love life's challenges, however challenging.

With love

X

*W*hat is it that you love most about you?

Is it your energy, your compassion, your health, your spirituality, your centredness, your thirst for knowledge, your strength, or something else?

Today, take a few moments during the day to ask yourself that question: "What is it that I love most about me?" Notice what comes up for you and how grateful you feel for whatever it is that comes up.

We are all truly remarkable bundles of energy. There is so much to love about ourselves. Sometimes we don't take the time to appreciate ourselves. Today take a few moments to do that.

With love

x

37

*P*eople come, people go. Experiences come, experiences go. Money comes, money goes. Possessions come, possessions go. Pretty well everything comes and everything goes.

So... What's the point?

What if the point is the journey? And more particularly, the journey of our soul? The soul that remains with us throughout our human experience, whilst everything else comes and goes... Our spirit remains.

But what of all our human achievements? Surely they are fantastic and amazing? Yes, but what if those achievements were there not for their own end, but rather to enable the soul to break through challenges and develop further? What if that were true?

When I ask "What's the point?", it's not because I believe there is no point. It's because I believe with my heart that there is a point but that the point might be different to that which we're conditioned to believe...

Something to think about.

With love

x

38

We have all we need to make every day the most amazing, awesome day.

Are all your days really amazing and awesome?

We so often settle for feeling "ok" or "all right" or "fine" or "good". How does that serve us when every moment of every day can feel awesome?

Every day presents challenges (a.k.a. growth opportunities). How we arrive at those challenges is entirely our choice. What's more, how we arrive at those challenges usually has a material impact on how we experience them and how much growth materialises.

We can decide to be awesome or outstanding or terrific, every moment of every day. How would that compare with feeling "ok" or "all right" or "fine" or "good"? Maybe we'd experience each moment of our day differently?

Today, decide to be awesome or outstanding. Don't settle for ok or good. Notice how it feels, how you feel about you and how you experience your day.

Try this too: When you're asked how you are today, reply "I'm awesome, thanks. How are you doing?" Notice how others respond...

Have an amazing day.

With love

x

39

So much fear and scarcity in the world...

Take a deep breath, find the reasons to be grateful in this moment, and let's transform the world one person at a time.

Let's lead the way by living in abundance. We all have experiences of how that works out even if we are conditioned to live in scarcity and fear.

Let's remember those times when we believed things, time, love, etc., were abundant and ask ourselves, did our experience match our belief? Did life feel better? Did our challenges feel more overcomeable (is that even a word?)?

Living in abundance is a choice, in that same way that living in fear and scarcity is a choice.

Choose wisely.

With love

x

40

*F*eeling the love that's inside all of us is one of the most beautiful, enriching and re-energising feelings we can experience on a day to day basis.

Feeling our own love enables us to better share love with everyone we encounter in our daily lives. It enriches the whole world.

How amazing, that by simply giving ourselves the gift of feeling the love that's inside of us, each of us will be enriching the world in which we live.

This is one of the ways we can contribute towards making the world a more loving place for everyone.

Today, for a few moments, sit quietly, breath deeply and slowly and feel the love inside of you. Let's make the world a more loving place.

With love

x

41

*L*ove everyone and everything.

That is my simple message today. Begin with yourself, feel your own love, radiate that love every moment of every day.

Notice how your energy, your relationships, your well-being, in fact everything feels better when you're radiating love.

With love

x

42

*F*ear and low self worth — both are so prominent in our society today. Yet the ways in which they manifest are diverse. The masks that they hide behind are designed to demonstrate the complete absence of fear and low self-worth. They are the masks of the ego.

As always, the answer is love, for us to love ourselves so that we can be love. Then our love will radiate from us, showing those whom we interact with that there is another way. Not only the way of the ego (which is 100% based on fear and low self-worth) but the way of love, compassion and gratitude.

Today, throughout the day, breathe into your heart and sense the feeling of love that is within you. It's always there, it always has been there and always will be there. Noticing that love and being grateful for that love diminishes the power of the ego until eventually the ego is powerless and we return to love.

With love

x

43

*T*here is so much more good going on in the world than we are led to believe. There is so much less to fear than we are led to believe. There is so much more love and compassion in the world than we're led to believe.

Yet if you tune into a current affairs show you are likely to "greeted" with:

Death

Murder

Scarcity

Violence

Blame

Every day we have the choice as to what we allow into our personal environment.

Choose wisely.

With love

x

44

*I*t's commonplace to believe that improving the world is in the hands of others: politicians, entrepreneurs, religious leaders, business leaders, spiritual leaders.

And we can easily get caught up living our lives, paying the bills, putting out the dustbins, cleaning the car, creating financial disasters, working long hours, breaking up, breaking down, etc., etc., etc.

But really, the awesome thing is that we can all improve the world right now. Simple acts such as smiling, holding a door open for someone, offering to help someone who has their hands full, nurturing a plant, etc., etc.

Today, grab hold of your opportunities to improve the world. It's our responsibility to improve the world, and once the movement of world improvement gains momentum it will be unstoppable, because our hearts will connect across the globe and that is an energy that is unbreakable.

Remember, it can be as simple as a smile...

With love

x

45

Someone once told me that it takes more effort to frown than it does to smile, so why not smile?

As with many things there is contradictory evidence available so who knows the truth?

My experience is that I feel better when I'm smiling than when I'm frowning, so that's as good a reason as any to smile. The best feeling is when the smile comes from the heart.

Try for yourself, smile from your heart and notice how that feels.

Then see how frowning from the heart works for you...

With love

x

46

*W*hat is love?

Lots of words are written and spoken but what really is the essence of love?

It's one of those questions that if you ask ten people you probably get at least eleven different answers.

To me the fundamental aspect of love is that love is unconditional. There are no strings attached, no expectations. What's more, if we don't love ourselves unconditionally then we will never truly love another.

The unconditional love of ourselves is liberating, it clears the path for our soul to express itself and find its purpose in this lifetime.

Start by loving yourself. At least start by not beating yourself up about all the stuff you haven't done or could have done better or wish you hadn't done. Be kind to you, love you every day and notice what happens.

With love

x

47

*L*et today be about love and connection. Just imagine, if everyone shared that intention today... Just imagine.

Start by loving yourself and then reconnect within someone you've lost touch with, maybe an old friend or a former work colleague or perhaps a relation. Reconnect with no agenda other than to connect.

You will be amazed at what follows. Not necessarily today or tomorrow, not necessarily directly with that person. Somehow, our intentions get recognised and amazing things follow.

Love and connection.

With love

x

48

*L*ook around. There is so much to appreciate and be grateful for. If you're struggling for things to appreciate and you're breathing, then that could be a start.

The preoccupation that most people have with "stuff" acts as a time-filling distraction away from what's really important.

What's important?

Being grateful, appreciating all that is available to us on a daily basis. All the relationships, the peace, the love — all of these are freely available. If you want to have stuff in your life then at least be sure that it's stuff like that!

Being grateful is an awesome place to start.

With love

x

49

*A*llow yourself the time and space in your life to play a little. As children, playing is an integral part of life.

We "grow up" and life somehow appears to be less playful, we get educated, get qualifications, get a job, get a car, get a partner, get a house, have a family, get a bigger car, get a bigger house, etc., etc., etc.

The secret is (just whisper this one because it will blow the minds of most people!) we can do all of those things whilst being playful.

It's true, we can continue to be playful throughout our lives! And an awesome consequence of being playful is that we get to do all the things (and more) that everybody else does and... we enjoy them more because we're being playful.

Today, be playful. How about skipping somewhere, or splashing in a puddle, or if you have children, playing with them, or caring less about outcome and just enjoying whatever it is you're doing for the pure fun of it?

Life is a playful journey. Remember to be playful.

With love

x

50

*B*e aware that we need to take care of our own business and allow everybody else the time and space to do the same. Through caring and wanting to be helpful we really are in danger of suffocating our development as humans.

What does that mean?

We learn most through active participation, in other words, by doing. Increasingly, I observe caring, loving, well intended people disrupt and destroy the learning process and with it the confidence and spirit of bright, sparkling individuals.

Please, please, please allow yourself the space to do and learn what you need to do and learn. The way to do that is to let everyone else get on with what they need to do and learn.

Become an observer and send people love, for that will enrich your life and those with whom you interact.

Finally, remember how children learn to walk? With love and support and by falling over! Parents cannot walk for their children... Something to think about.

With love

x

51

*G*etting into our flow, that feeling of bliss, all begins with being present.

We can only be blissful and flow in this moment. The next moment has yet to arrive and the previous moment has gone. It's this moment where our power lies.

Today, let's give ourselves the gift of being truly present whilst doing everyday tasks such as cleaning our teeth, washing dishes, taking a shower, traveling to work, etc., etc.

Stop the flow of thoughts and just be present, feel the toothbrush as it moves across every tooth, notice how the dishes sparkle and shine once washed, feel the water from the shower as it cascades over your body, notice the beauty of your natural surroundings on your journey to work.

Just for a few moments immerse yourself and notice how that feels. The present moment is the only moment we have and being truly present is where we find our flow and feel blissful.

Have a beautiful day.

With love

x

52

*E*xplore and enjoy exploring your creativity. As children, our creativity is largely un-constrained, yet we move into adulthood and our creativity tends to get smothered by the demands of others (though remember it's our choice how we respond to any external demands... but that's for another day).

Continuing to revel in our creativity is where we will find so much of life's beautiful offerings.

Personally, I believed for years (and I mean 40+ years) that I simply wasn't creative. What a load of nonsense. Everyone is creative, we all have creativity within us and the world is a better place when more people acknowledge and share their creativity. My personal experience is that since my creativity has been revealed the level of pleasure in and around my life is just awesome. What's more, it has benefited me and all those I interact with

I am grateful that my creativity is flourishing and my wish for you is that however creative you believe you are right now, start believing that you're even more creative. Enjoy!

With love

x

53

*B*eing grateful is transformative for you and everyone you interact with.

A few moments of our day sitting in gratitude... It's impossible to describe how it feels and the value it adds but really, the only way to experience it is to be grateful.

Today, for a few moments/minutes sit, close your eyes, focus on your breathing. As you notice your breathing, the thoughts rushing through your head will slow. Then, be grateful from your heart, sit with that gratitude and breath slowly and deeply. Just for a few moments (though longer is definitely allowed).

Notice how you feel as you go through your day and notice how your interactions with others are transformed.

With love

X

54

*L*ive today with a skip in your step and a smile in your heart. That's how it was when we were children and for most of us life then was a little more carefree and adventurous

If challenges come along, then remember that challenges are gifts that enable us to grow. Welcome challenges with a skip and a smile

Have an awesome day.

With love

x

55

*L*ive your life to the maximum.

By living your life to the maximum you'll be a shining beacon for all those that interact with you.

The positive impacts are way beyond our comprehension. The impacts continue far, far beyond our immediate environment and lifetime. Imagine that: the way we are has impacts beyond our human lifetime. How mind-blowing is that?

Share your joy, spread your light and live your life... every day.

With love

x

56

*R*emember that life is much simpler than we've been led to believe.

Every day there are people whose egos want them to tell everyone how clever they are because they understand some aspect of the complexities of human life. It's all nonsense; life is simple, it's meant to be simple and it's only we humans who complicate it... because we think we're so clever!

We need to get over ourselves and enjoy the simple pleasures in life, because there is an abundance of beauty and miracles surrounding us every day.

If you find your ego buying into the complexities of life, just remember that life is simple. In that moment stop, look around and identify whatever beauty and miracles happen to be within view. Enjoy the moment, return your ego to its place and continue with your day.

With love

x

57

*S*implification... the key to a truly successful life.

As humans we are extremely intelligent creatures, but with that intelligence comes an ability to over-engineer and over-complicate our lives because we like to stretch our capabilities.

Think today where you can simplify your life. This will leave space for your vast intelligence to explore new and exciting subjects and activities, just for the pleasure of it.

Simplification really is a gift — explore and enjoy it today and every day.

With love

x

58

*R*emember to take care of you.

Take care of your health during this human lifetime. Without health and energy our lives are compromised. And please remember that fitness and health are very different, and of the two, health is by far the most important.

Be kind to you too. It's all too easy to find ways to beat ourselves up, to be hard on ourselves, to focus on what we've not done. Give yourself a break, share your love with yourself. Recognise all the amazing contributions you've made to your life and to the lives of so many others.

You're awesome... Remember?

With love

x

59

*S*o much of the hurt and pain in the world is self-induced. By simply loving and respecting ourselves we start to reduce our own hurt and pain.

There are many occasions where our internal dialogue is such that if someone else spoke to us in that way we'd probably never speak with them again! What's more we'd never speak to others the way we speak to ourselves when we're giving ourselves a hard time for all the things we haven't done or what we've done wrong.

The truth is that life is a reflection. One aspect of that is that the way we interact with others is consistent with the way we interact with ourselves. In other words, if we don't love and respect ourselves, then we cannot truly love and respect others. We will probably be polite with others but until we truly love and respect ourselves we will not truly love and respect others.

Imagine how the world would be if we were kind to ourselves, if we loved and respected ourselves. We would all naturally then be kind to, love and respect others. Our relationships would blossom!

With love

x

60

Maintaining balance in our lives, in all aspects of our lives, leads to greater contentment and peace in our lives, which is fab. The ripple effects of living balanced lives are far reaching and transformational.

Yet balance is not something that is commonly a priority. Increasingly, intense/extreme approaches are adopted to enable us to maintain balance in our lives. Surely there is a conflict.

Perhaps the truth is that our lives, the lives of those we interact with and therefore the world would be better if we committed to taking small steps every day to maintain balance in our lives. If every day we did something to nurture our mind, our body and our spirit, the ripple effect through our whole life would be beautiful.

It only needs to take a few minutes every day. Give yourself the gift of nurturing your mind, body and spirit. Notice how it feels to nurture the balance in you.

With love

x

61

*H*ead vs. Heart

So often we'll hear the expression "my head says one thing but my heart says something else". Invariably this can be interpreted to mean "I'd love what my heart says to happen but I'm certain that it won't so I'll listen to my head".

Why do we continue to compromise and limit the joy in our life? Our heart knows best. If more people followed their heart just imagine how much joy there would be in the world.

Don't follow the crowd, follow your heart. Your heart ALWAYS knows best.

With love

x

*L*isten to you, your intuition, your heart. That's where all the wisdom you'll ever need for this life sits, so please listen.

Follow a hunch, go on gut feeling, listen to that something inside you. However your intuition manifests itself, be aware, notice, listen and act upon it.

Our hearts, not our heads, hold all the wisdom we need.

With love

x

63

Nurturing ourselves and our relationships, being nurturing enriches lives beyond measure.

We never really know the full extent of our impact in the world. A simple smile to a stranger can change their feeling in that moment, which can lead to a change of direction in their day and the lives of those they interact with. Equally a frown to a stranger could be just as impactful though not necessarily with the same set of outcomes.

If we nurture ourselves and nurture our relationships then our sense of well-being is enhanced. And if we feel better about ourselves, then just imagine what that could lead to.

Keep life simple. Today, give yourself the gift of a nurturing day, notice how that feels and feel free to do it again tomorrow and for as many days as you choose!

With love

x

64

*W*ishing you a playful day. Today and every day.

As children we are regularly encouraged to play, to create and to enjoy adventures. As we move out of childhood to become youths and then adults we tend to be encouraged/ guided/conditioned to get an education, earn a living, settle down. Gradually the balance of our life tends to transition from playful, adventurous creativity to studying, paying the bills, living for the weekend or the annual vacation.

Somewhere along the way many people's sparkle is diminished. Today, give your sparkle more life; being playful brings more life to your sparkle. Have a playful day. It will lift your spirit and enable your sparkle to shine

With love

x

65

*D*uring our day-to-day activities, how often do we pause, breathe and consciously notice the beauty and miracles that surround us?

Just to pause for a few moments and to breathe slowly and deeply is in itself a gift. To also let our attention wander to all around us that we can be grateful for amplifies that gift beyond measure.

Today, give yourself the beautiful gift of some moments when you consciously notice the beauty and miracles that surround you every moment of every day. You will naturally find yourself being grateful, which on its own is transformative

With love

x

66

*F*orming love-based relationships is one of the great joys of life. Humans thrive on heartfelt, loving relationships. The healthiest relationships are those where there are no expectations, no conditions.

So often relationships are created based on a perceived need or desire, where one party sees the relationship (often not at a conscious level) as an interaction from which they will benefit. In other words, the relationship is seen as a trade: I'll trade you some time and attention on the expectation that you'll hire me, or you'll introduce me to someone I want to meet, or you'll do something for me...

Contrast that basis for a relationship with a relationship based on love and acceptance. In these relationships, both people enter into the relationship for the pure joy of connecting with another loving being. There is no other motive; it's all about coming from a loving place.

As we continue to form our human relationships, let's do so from this loving place. Let's enter into each relationship focusing on what we bring to the relationship rather than what we'd like to get from the relationship. Then we'll see our relationships blossom.

With love

x

67

*A*ll our dreams really do come true. Believe in your dreams, believe in yourself, believe that there is always a way.

So often our dreams become compromised or dumbed down through the conditioning and fear that dominates the world today. There are so many well-meaning people who contribute to the compromising of dreams.

Witness this exchange between a bright teenager and his careers advisor, which went along the lines of:

Careers advisor: "What are you planning to do once you've completed education?"

Teenager: "Be a professional golfer, an actor or a magician."

Careers advisor: "That's all very well, but you'll need to get a proper job."

In that moment the colour drained from the teenager's face as this well-meaning careers advisor took a swipe at the dreams of the teenager.

That type of interaction is taking place every day, thousands of time a day. Ask yourself, in what way is that serving the world?

Believe that your dreams will come true, believe that anything is possible and wish the well-meaning fear mongerers a good day as you follow your dreams.

As a conclusion to the interaction above, the careers advisor is still advising on careers. The teenager has completed his education and is forging his career as a magician performing at parties, weddings, charity events, etc., etc.

There is always a way.

With love

x

Tim Brister

68

We live in a world where what we do and what we achieve tends to be recognised and rewarded. Yet it's our way of being that is far more important in determining our life satisfaction levels.

There are many examples of high-achieving "successful" people from many walks of life, and many of these people have done some remarkable things. However, many of these people have shown themselves to be dissatisfied with their human existence.

Instead of doing, let's adjust the emphasis of our life, let's decide on our way of being. For we do have the power to decide in every moment.

We can be anything we choose. We can be loving, caring, angry, sad, happy, content, frustrated, creative... What would you choose to be?

From our chosen way of being, we will be able to achieve. However, by choosing our way of being, our way of being is independent of whatever we do.

What a concept... It doesn't matter what we do/achieve; our state of being is entirely up to us to choose. Despite what we may have been led to believe, we don't have to achieve anything to be whatever we want.

Just think about that...

Enjoy being whatever you want to be.

With love

x

69

*T*here is so much to enjoy and so much to marvel about. Why then, do we "mature" as humans, and as we mature, why do we tend to dwell less on the miracles and wonders of life? Instead we choose to pay attention to what goes on in the "real" world...

What is really real? The miracles and wonders of life or the reality we experience as we mature?

The truth is that we create our own reality. For example, a group of people can participate in exactly the same event yet come away with completely different experiences. Which experience is real? For each individual their own experience is reality; each individual has created their own reality.

Be aware that we are all creating our own reality, every moment of every day. Why not choose to create a reality that is going to be empowering, supportive and magical?

Choose wisely.

With love

x

*L*iving every day with vibrant health and energy might seem like a far-off dream, a way of living for others who have more time to train, others who have more money to eat healthier food, others who are naturally healthy.

Living with vibrant health and energy is our birthright; it's our natural way of being. Without doubt, there will still be times where our bodies need to handle disease, but when our bodies are vibrant with health and energy, the disease will be handled.

There are three main components to leading a healthy and vibrant life: what we do with our bodies (exercise etc.); how we fuel our bodies (food, drink, etc.); and finally the most important element, how we treat ourselves (being kind to ourselves, loving ourselves, taking emotional care of ourselves, etc.).

Whilst we might be able to come up with excuses as to why we don't exercise regularly and why we don't consistently eat in a healthy way, being kind and loving to ourselves is simply a choice that we make in every moment of every day. It requires no time, no money, no special equipment or ingredients.

Imagine that you can enhance your levels of health and energy through a simple choice to love yourself unconditionally...

We really are truly amazing beings.

With love

x

71

*A*ccepting and being grateful for our life today does not mean that we want our lives to remain exactly as they are forever. In nature there is growing and there is dying; there is no way to stand still. All plants, flowers, trees are either growing or dying. It is the same for us humans.

So why would we accept or be grateful for our life today and why is that important? Gratitude is transformative: The more grateful we are, the more we attract people, events, experiences into our life that we enjoy and therefore enable us to feel greater gratitude.

It's an amazing place to be. Being grateful leads us to notice more things to be grateful for, which then increases the abundance in our lives because we continue to be aware of more and more things to be grateful for. All of which leads us to being more grateful and abundant.

Simply put, the very act of being grateful puts us in a place of growth and abundance.

Today, be grateful — every moment of the day.

With love

x

72

*W*hat we focus on is what we get. The Law of Attraction talks about thoughts becoming things. What we think about on a consistent basis will manifest in our lives.

Take a moment to look at where and what you focus on. So often we focus on what we haven't done, what didn't go well, what could be improved. Often the purpose for this focus is in order for us to learn and improve. And there is certainly a time and place for learning and improving.

However, for many of us, we never take time to look at all the amazing things we have done, the ways in which we've cared for others, the love we've shared, the books we've read, the awesome work we've done, the commitment to our family... The list goes on and on and on.

Striking a balance is key. It's important that we reflect on areas, events, relationships in our lives where we've got the opportunity to learn and develop. However, remember to invest more time and energy to reflect on areas, events, and relationships in our lives where we've made massive contributions and feel proud of what we've done and who we've been.

One way to improve that balance in our lives is at the end of the day to make a note of at least 3-5 things from our day that we're proud of. Soon it will become second nature and start to rebalance the feelings that we have about ourselves and our lives.

And guess what: The more we focus on things we've done that we feel proud of, the more things we'll do that make us feel proud of ourselves.

With love

x

Tim Brister

73

*T*he life of our dreams might appear to be a dream that will never manifest into our human existence.

If we allow our dreams to become overtaken by "being realistic" or getting a "real job" or any number of man-made obstacles, then our dreams will not manifest.

But — just look around at everything that humans have created. All of those creations began with a dream, a dream held by dreamers who carried on pursuing their dreams until they manifested.

Just think, who would have believed it realistic to fly, to walk on the moon, to be able to communicate across the globe with tiny devices smaller than our hands, to run a mile in less than four minutes, etc. All of these were once viewed as impossible dreams.

Love your dreams, nurture your dreams, believe in your dreams and let the miracles of the universe unfold.

Keep dreaming.

With love

x

74

*K*now that we are all here on this earth for a reason. Know that you are a special, unique being. Most of all, know your worth, your value and be comfortable with your worth.

This beautiful world is populated with such a diverse set of beings. Collectively we form the consciousness of the planet. We are that single consciousness.

As an aside, we are a single consciousness, so every conflict, every argument, every war is an internal conflict, argument, war with ourselves. Consider that...

Whilst we are a single consciousness, we remain humans with our own uniqueness and contribution. Respect yourself, know that you are unique and that only you can bring the value and worth that you bring.

Others are likely to disrespect your value and worth, in the same way that they disrespect their own value and worth. Send them love and wish them well as you continue on your unique path. There are always people out there who will understand your value and worth, because they understand their value and worth.

The first thing is to value your uniqueness and believe in your worth. Then notice how many others you meet who similarly have respect for their own (and your) value and worth.

With love

x

Tim Brister

75

*B*elieve that everything is perfect just as it is... because it is as it is. It is easy to believe that our circumstances aren't perfect, our relationships aren't perfect, our neighbours aren't perfect, our work isn't perfect, and so on and so on.

Accepting what is, accepting that every moment is perfect and being grateful for everything that is does not mean that we stop developing or that our life journey ends. Quite the opposite, accepting the perfection of every moment and being grateful for every moment is the very thing that creates the freedom of expression within us to live our life with joy, health and love.

Let go of judgement; let go of ungratefulness; love the perfection of every moment to enable your heart and soul to sing and dance with joy!

With love

x

*T*aking care of ourselves has many levels. One of the tragedies in the world is that most people only start to really take care of themselves following some kind of life event, health issue or something similar. Taking care of ourselves on a daily basis enables us to live our lives to the full, at every level.

Take care of the whole of you: your mind, body and soul.

Move your body every day and eat a healthy, balanced diet. The simple guidelines of eat less and move more are a great start.

Look after your mind, continue to learn throughout life and take care of the thoughts you allow to persist in your mind. It's our choice what we think about.

Feed and support your soul through love. Love yourself first; love everyone, always.

With love

x

77

*A*dventure, exploration and discovery: three activities that bring variety into our life. How much of each do you have in your life?

Some of us vision adventure as camping in the Amazon rain forest or climbing Everest. For many of us, that vision of adventure is more daunting than our idea of adventure.

Adventure can be as simple as going out for a walk with friends in a part of town that we don't know or taking a completely different route to work or taking a vacation to a city you've never been to before.

It's easy, as our life progresses, to imagine that things such as exploration, adventure and discovery are major undertakings that we'll never get to enjoy. Did we have that view as children or was every day an adventure for exploration and discovery?

We didn't need to go to the Amazon or climb Everest as children — there was adventure in every moment.

Treat every day as a day of adventure, exploration and discovery.

With love

x

78

As we go through life there is a tendency to acquire and hold on to "baggage". Maybe some regrets, missed opportunities, bad investments, lost friendships, etc. This baggage feels pretty heavy after a while, especially as we tend to accumulate it and never let go of any. It gets heavier and heavier.

Let's go back to a time when we didn't have all this baggage, a time when we were carefree, a time when life was lighter, laughter-filled and adventurous. For most people that sounds like parts of our childhood.

Today, let's reclaim those feelings of adventure, of being carefree, of joy. Let's fearlessly explore and learn about something new that excites us. Let's see how that feels, how our spirits are lifted, how we feel lighter, how we skip with joy!

Do something today that makes your heart sing. Forget the baggage and live with passion.

With love

x

*E*nergy flows within us and around us constantly. There is always an abundance of energy in the world. A question for us is how much of that energy is available to us at any given moment.

Feeling like we don't have any energy is a feeling we've all experienced from time to time. By nurturing our mind, body and spirit we can get to a place of having a consistently abundant level of energy, so we never need have that feeling of no energy again.

There are many ways in which we can get to that place of consistently abundant energy. Here are some nurturing ideas:

We can nurture our body through the gifts of sleep, exercise, good nutritious food.

We can nurture our minds through continued learning, meditation, stimulating dialogue.

We can nurture our souls by being at one with nature, by listening to our heart, by being present in every moment.

You'll soon see that all of these ideas link together and produce momentum in all aspects of the mind, body and soul. For example, meditation benefits the mind, body and soul, as does being at one with nature, as does the gift of sleep.

The thing to do is to nurture yourself, start the ball rolling and watch as the power of momentum leads to massive

transformations in your life and particularly the energy levels you feel.

Start with just one nurturing activity, then another, then another...

With love

x

80

*T*he level of connection and quality of interaction with others is so much deeper and more powerful once we have truly connected with ourselves. Of all the connections we make during our lifetimes, the foundational connection is with ourselves.

What does it mean to connect with ourselves? It's about a feeling of peace, of being centred, trusting our instincts, and it's about loving ourselves, accepting that we must connect with us first before we are able to truly connect with others.

Give yourself and the world the gift of you listening to yourself, giving yourself space to be, you loving yourself just as you are in every moment. You deserve it.

With love

x

81

*A*llowing ourselves to be, just as we are, without self-criticism, without self-judgement or self-doubt is one of the most beautiful gifts we can give to ourselves. When we allow ourselves to be, to be present in this moment as love, all our ego-driven shackles fall away. We truly disarm our ego.

The ego is determined, persistent and cunning. Its sole purpose is to survive and it can only survive by keeping us distracted from the present moment (through the creation of the past and future) and to create and then maintain a disconnect with our heart and soul (by keeping us in our head).

Therefore, our allowing ourselves to be in each moment is a moment by moment activity, not a one-off event. It's a bit like improving our strength/fitness: we don't go to the gym once and believe that we're done for life; we keep going to the gym if we want to be stronger/fitter.

Enjoy every moment, connect with every moment and allow yourself to be in every moment. And when the ego pops up with it's tricks and distractions, notice what's happening, let it go, and return to being in that moment.

Remember always that the present moment is the only moment we ever have.

With love

x

82

A simple smile lights up not only the face of the smiler but reflects on all those around. We never know how far the ripples of our smile's impact spread.

At the very moment we smile, there could be someone nearby who picks up on the energy behind the smile. For some reason unknown to them, they begin to feel a spark of energy where they felt none before. That spark of energy could lead to a state of being which leads that person to take any number of actions, perhaps planting a tree, giving a loved one a hug, applying for a job, smiling at others (without any awareness of the ripples)...

We can begin to see how the ripples of our simple smile can spread way beyond our awareness. What a beautiful thing.

Smile.

With love

x

83

*L*iving the life of our dreams has nothing to do with big houses, fast cars or worldly possessions. Living the life of our dreams comes about when we truly listen to our heart, when our soul is free to express itself.

There is a lot of human fun to be had with holidays, fast cars, worldly possessions, etc., but these are not what our heart dreams about. Our heart dreams about being heard. The magical thing is that once our heart is being heard, then human fun flows with abundance (with or without the worldly toys and possessions).

Our heart speaks in feelings, not words. Allow yourself to be open, connected to yourself and the feelings of your heart. Let those feelings flow and your life will be transformed.

With love

x

84

*L*isten to your heart, always listen to your heart. You may not always be able to figure out what your heart is saying, but that's ok.

The heart needs to feel listened to even when the messages are not obvious to us humans. Simply enabling the heart to speak and letting the messages of the heart know they are being heard is enough.

Our heart has many ways to ensure its messages have impact; our choice is whether we listen. It is the listening that empowers the messages of the heart.

With love

x

*T*here is much in the world today that is out of alignment. Witness the civil unrest, the regular appearance of new deadly diseases, terrorism and wars. The paradox is that the peace and connection that is absent in the world already exists inside all of us; we just need to rediscover it.

Imagine a world where everyone is at ease with themselves, is loving themselves and listening to their heart. Imagine a world where everyone cares for and nurtures relationships and where everyone is contributing to a worldwide collaborative effort to nurture the whole planet. Imagine that.

There would be no war, disease would not be able to thrive, love would be everywhere and everything.

Some would say that vision is a pipe dream. But remember, we all have the possibility to move the world towards that more loving, peaceful, connected space. The way to do that is for each of us to be love, to be peace, to be connected.

Imagine.

With love

x

86

*L*isten to, feel and sense the messages and signals that the universe is offering every day. Keeping our minds quiet, listening with our heart and trusting that the universe has our back will transform our lives and the lives of those we are connected to and as a consequence raise the vibration of everyone on the planet

There is a certain magical beauty in this whole process of raising vibration, yet in truth, there is no magic to it at all. Deep down we know what to do. In our heart, we know what to do.

With love

x

87

*W*hen we feel challenged or something that doesn't resonate with us is presented to us, then it's easy to dismiss that as wrong because we feel that our position is right for us. Rather than dismissing the challenge as wrong, embrace it. There is a reason why that particular challenge has come into our life at this moment.

As our human existence extends, then we can easily become more certain about our feelings on a whole bunch of topics. Often, the more certain we become, the less open we are to different points of view. Yet our spiritual growth and freedom is accelerated when we embrace and learn from challenges to our feelings of certainty.

Sometimes situations that challenge us lead us to understand better what causes us to feel so certain. The challenges don't necessarily lead to us coming to a different sense of certainty but the very process of embracing the challenge causes us to grow.

Welcome and embrace challenge. If something feels uncomfortable, be grateful and ask yourself what there is for you to learn from this challenge.

With love

x

88

*B*eing true to yourself, living the truth of who you are, letting your truth shine through. However we articulate it, there is one simple way to be true and that is to listen to our heart. Our heart knows our truth.

The depth of connectedness we feel when we are living our truth is blissful. We feel like we're in the flow of our life. We've all felt that from time to time. Connecting with and listening to our heart enables us to live in that flow where every moment feels like a blessing.

Check in with yourself on a regular basis. Ask, does this feel right to me? Do I feel any discomfort with this? What is niggling away at me about this? All those types of questions are checking in with your truth, your heart.

Whenever we feel discomfort or unease then it's a good indication that there's some misalignment between what we're doing/being and our truth.

Live from your heart and feel your truth.

With love

x

89

*D*oes humanity know what it's doing? Observe the world leaders (political, religious, business, terrorist) with their fear-based rhetoric, further fuelled by the world's (social) media.

The key, common thread is that the leaders largely operate out of fear — and where is the love in that? The answer is that there is no love in fear!

Fear leads to hate, to uncertainty, to war, to doubt. Is that really where humanity wants to head towards? Ask yourself how the leaders of the world could lead humanity away from love.

But there is a change afoot, from the ground up. More and more people are feeling dis-satisfied. They may not know why or what to do about it but the feeling is spreading.

We (the human race) are remembering that it's about what we are being, not what we are doing. And then we're remembering it's about being love.

It's down to every one of us to help humanity to remember that being love is the way for humanity to leave behind the pain of living in a world dominated by fear.

Follow your heart.. Love.

With love

x

90

*T*here often appears to be a preconception that we in some way need fixing, in other words, we are broken. This is so far from the truth.

We are perfect in every way. What's more, we are always doing the best we can based on where we are and what we know. This concept of being broken largely comes from external referencing. It's just not true!

Any comparison of ourself with anything outside of ourself is completely irrelevant, pointless and usually destructive. Next time you find yourself comparing any part of your life with something or someone else, notice how that feels inside of you.

Simply remember that you are perfect; we are all perfect with our imperfections. Love yourself as you are.

With love

x

91

*L*iving a life being loving, passionate and grateful is where we'll find our flow. Living a life being fearful, suppressed and ungrateful is where we'll find our pain and feel stuck.

When expressed in that way, the choice appears simple, and indeed the choice is simple. However, the (unconscious) choice of most people is to live in pain! Look around...

How can that be?

All around us there are miracles, there is joy, there is untold beauty, yet much of the daily conditioning in our man-made environment is based on fear, suppression and guilt.

Be aware. Choose your thoughts and feelings based on love, not fear. Then you're in flow and the world becomes an even more beautiful experience for everyone.

With love

x

*A*lways remember, it's not what you say or what you do that people remember.

What people remember are the feelings and emotions that they feel during and after interactions with you.

Every moment of every day we have the choice as to our state of being. The state of being we choose is the most powerful influence over our level of contentment with our lives, which in turn impacts hugely on the emotions and feelings others feel when interacting with us.

The more we are being centred, loving, connected, and joyful, the more likely we are to be present with ourselves and with others. Being present is when true magic happens.

Be present in every moment and listen to the wisdom of your heart.

With love

x

*C*onnecting with our dreams, our passion, the joy of life transforms our human experience. It's so easy to get caught up in making a living or getting by that we forget that life is a gift to be enjoyed.

When we are living in the flow of our passion, then our life experiences shift to a feeling of bliss, peace and joy.

Live your passion, follow your dreams and spread your light as you flow through life. Watch as those around you follow your lead — now, that's magical.

With love

x

94

 We are blessed to live in an abundant world. The abundance in the world manifests for each of us to the extent that we are connected and living in flow.

Living in flow and being connected might sound daunting, strange, even impossible. The truth is that living in flow and being connected come about naturally when we are loving and grateful.

Being love and gratitude are the keys that unlock so many doors for us.

With love

x

95

*L*isten to your inner voice, your heart, your soul — whichever description resonates with you.

Because one thing is for sure, not listening to our inner voice causes disease in our body. Sometimes that disease is relatively minor, but if we repeatedly ignore the wisdom of our inner voice, then the inner voice finds a way to express itself through major disease/trauma.

Take care of you. Listen to your inner voice.

With love

x

96

*L*ove the awesome perfection of our human existence. Every day we collectively co-create our experiences. Those experiences are always the perfect experiences in that moment.

From time to time our experiences are uncomfortable and/ or challenging. Be certain that these are the experiences that we need at that moment.

Be grateful for every moment, for every experience, and trust that whatever is happening for you in your life, it's perfect.

Perfection.

With love

x

97

*I*f you are ever wondering about when the most opportune moment is, the answer is simple. We always have only one moment and that moment is now.

We deserve to immerse ourselves, to relish, to be truly alive (not just existing) in every moment. In those moments our contribution to the world is aligned with our true purpose and there's magic in that moment, not just for us but for everyone.

We never know the impacts of our thoughts, feelings and actions. What we can be sure of is that the impacts reach far further than we can ever imagine.

Thoughts, feelings and actions that arise from our soul, i.e. when we are aligned with our true purpose, are going to reach just as far as thoughts that don't arise from our soul. It's our choice. Which would you choose?

With love

x

98

*B*eing truly present in each moment might sound easy, but it's easy to become distracted as our minds wander.

Our wandering mind is really our ego taking us away from the present. Our ego has no power in the present; ego only has power in the past and the future.

What our ego then does is encourages us to give ourselves a hard time for not being in the present. It's just a trick of the ego to continue to keep us out of the present by focusing on past moments!

Live in the present, this moment right now, the only one we truly have. When you notice you've drifted away from the present, be grateful for having noticed and reconnect with the present. No sign of ego at all, no sign of giving yourself a hard time, just living in the present and being grateful.

With love

x

*T*he inner peace and calm that comes when we listen to ourselves is a thing of beauty. Our inner voice holds all the wisdom we need; we just need to listen to it.

When our inner voice speaks, many times we need to hear the same message multiple times before we listen. Yet if we hear an "expert" speaking, often someone we don't know, then we are prone to act... Something to think about.

Listen to the wisdom of your inner voice, your heart, your gut. The wisdom of our inner voice is awesome, but the strength of inner connection and peace we feel when we do listen to our inner voice, that is transformational.

With love

x

100

*T*here is so much emphasis on what we do, what we've done, what we are achieving. The truth is that we are on this earth to be; it is our being that really makes the biggest difference.

As humans we are creatures that take action, we do. And the doing tends to be more widely visible than the being.

However, it is our way of being that determines how content we are; it is not what we've done, nor what we've achieved, nor what we've accumulated.

Whether we're being loving, grateful, present or perhaps being vengeful, ungrateful, unloving, our state of being is at the root of our level of contentment.

We're going to do stuff, so we might as well choose to be loving, grateful, present, and do stuff from a place of being that supports us.

With love

x

*B*e grateful for everything in your life, even those events, those things, those people that don't necessarily feel comfortable.

Everything is a gift, every person is an angel. How could you not be grateful for gifts and angels?

Even physical pain is a gift. It might not feel like a gift but it truly is, so we might as well accept it as a gift and be grateful for the gift

Being grateful is transformative. Being grateful enables our light to shine bright, and that truly is a gift for everyone.

With love

x

*T*here is a lovely sentiment behind the saying "be thankful for small mercies". How about we expand that to "be thankful (for everything)".

Recently I saw a couple of boys aged around 10-11 walking around a park with a tray of muffins. They were going up to people, talking for a short period of time and moving on. As they approached me I was intrigued to hear their story.

It turns out, their local play area had been burned down (again). Rather than sit around and focus on the burning down of the play area these boys had some muffins baked and were in the park asking for donations to contribute towards the rebuilding of the play area in exchange for muffins.

From a situation that would have been miserable for many 10- or 11-year-olds — how is it when the area that you play in gets taken away? — these boys created a situation of thankfulness. They were thankful for the donations, and the donors were thankful for the opportunity to donate (and the muffins!).

Being thankful is a way of being. Everything, every experience, every person presents an opportunity to be thankful.

With love

x

103

*L*ife is a journey to be savoured, a journey of remembering who we are. All of the focus on results and achievement often leads us away from that truth about life being a journey to be enjoyed.

It starts so young, the pressure and focus on children to pass school exams and get grades. Our life is for fun, for play, for discovery. That's especially true of childhood, yet even in childhood we collectively lead our children away from the adventure that is life's journey.

Notice how your experience changes when you let go of the outcome and decide to simply enjoy the process, to enjoy the journey of your life. Try it today, enjoy the journey through your day.

With love

x

*L*ive and love from your heart. Listen to your heart. Trust your heart's wisdom.

Being heartfelt in everything you say, do, think, feel is a beautiful way to be. The world needs more of us to be heartfelt, for all of us

Be a heartfelt being and spread your light.

With love

x

105

*W*e are born as perfect, sparkling beings. We are perfect, every moment of our life.

Our human existence presents us with events, people, experiences that can lead us to accumulating emotional "stuff". Most of us allow our "stuff" to diminish our sparkle.

The truth is that we never lose our sparkle; it simply gets dulled by our "stuff".

One thing is for sure: However big, difficult, scary our stuff appears to be, we'll look back and wonder what we were thinking about when we allowed our stuff to dull our sparkle.

Instead of looking back and wondering, decide today to be the perfect, sparkling being that entered this human existence. And why not be even more sparkling than ever before?

Our perfection and sparkle never leaves us. It's our choice as to how much of our sparkle we experience and share.

Wishing you all a sparkling life!

With love

x

*O*ur human lives are adventures, our human powers and abilities are awesome. However, nothing compares with the power of the light of our soul.

Enjoy the human experience of this lifetime, but remember, the experience and journey of the soul is where the power of our existence lies.

With love

x

*Q*uieting our ego enables us to live in the moment. The ego has many subtle ways to keep us away from being present.

One of the ego's methods is judgement. Judgement never comes from a place of love; it's from the ego. Love is not judgemental.

Yet we learn about right and wrong very early in our human existence, so we assume that judgement is just something that we humans do. But it doesn't have to be that way; there is no judgement in love.

Observe and love. There's no ego there — just love.

With love

x

108

*A*s we collectively awaken and remember all that we have forgotten, it will be gratitude that emerges as the predominant way of being around the globe.

Through gratitude we quieten the noise of the ego. Through gratitude we are present in this moment, which is the only moment we ever have.

Being grateful truly is an experience like no other. Gratitude and love sit together perfectly; there is no space for the agenda of the ego.

Be grateful for everything, absolutely everything, and feel the love.

With love

x

More and more clearly, the path to enlightenment, to truly loving ourselves unconditionally is through being grateful for everything. Being grateful from the core of our being for the universe and every experience, every person, every feeling... everything.

Being grateful for everything can feel like a huge undertaking — after all, not everything feels good in the moment. That is true whilst we are being human and our egos are substantially influencing our human experience.

Start by being grateful for the sun, the rain, the grass, the umbrella that keeps you dry, the smartphone that keeps you connected, the food in your fridge, etc., etc., etc. The more we are grateful for things in our life that feel good, the more we move towards being grateful for everything.

Being grateful is transforming humanity. As more and more humans become grateful at their core, the more love and connection there is in the world. That is transformative.

With love

x

110

*L*oving yourself for being you is a gift of unbounded value to you and to everyone you interact with.

Loving yourself not only enables you to hear your heart, it is you listening to your heart.

Love is all there is.

With love

x

*T*he awesomeness of the universe and the perfection of every moment is just a joy to behold.

It might not always feel that way when we are presented with physical, emotional, financial, relationship challenges. But every challenge arrives at the perfect moment for us to remember what we need to remember at that moment.

Very often the challenges enable us to experience contrast so that we can better know, receive and appreciate that which we need. After all, how do we recognise light? Only through the existence of dark can we truly recognise light.

Similarly with health. Only through the absence of health do we really recognise perfect health.

Similarly with finances. The way we recognise financial abundance is through the experience of not being financially abundant.

These contrasts don't feel comfortable but the contrast is what enables us to truly recognise and appreciate that which we seek.

With love

x

Tim Brister

112

*W*e are always in exactly the right place at exactly the right time. This is something that many of us find hard to believe but it really is true.

Even when we're "certain" that we're not meant to be where we are with the people that we're with… we are. It might be that we're there to truly acknowledge our feelings of not belonging so that we make choices that are better aligned to our needs. That would be a fabulous reason for us to be where we are.

The important thing is to be sufficiently connected with ourselves to notice what we are feeling and to be grateful for the experience we are having.

With love

x

*L*ive your life! Live fearlessly with love in your heart and gratitude in your every thought.

For many of us, so much of our life is lived in fear, without gratitude or love. Immediately our ego will contradict that statement because our ego wants to keep us in fear, without gratitude or love.

Our ego thrives by keeping us fearful. The biggest fear it's created for us is the fear of death. What a great way to keep someone fearful: by making them become fearful of the one certain event within the human experience!

Drop the fear (it's all made up). Be gratitude and love. Live your life!

With love

x

114

*D*rop the judgement and simply love. And most important of all, begin with yourself. Stop judging yourself and simply love yourself.

We inhabit a world where judgement has become the norm, where judgement exists so pain, fear and ego are found.

Where judgement exists, love does not. Love does not judge, love simply loves.

Love yourself, be kind to yourself. Give yourself a break and stop judging yourself. Then you will notice that you become less judgemental of others. All of which means less judgement in the world.

Less judgement means there is more space for love

With love

x

*T*here is so much to do, so much we can do. Remember though that the most important thing is to be, whether we're being gratitude, being love, being peace, being serenity, etc.

We're blessed to live in a world at a time where there is so much that we could do. We can do the ironing, do the cleaning, do the budgeting. We can do paid work, do charity work, do voluntary work. We can take a vacation, we can chill out, we can do exercise, we can do some reading. The list is endless.

And whilst there's nothing wrong with all of that doing, the quality of our doing is wholly dependent on our state of being.

Being love or being gratitude will lead to a far different experience than if we are being frustrated or being angry.

Choose your way of being first. Watch your experiences transform.

With love

x

116

Make today a day of joy, of fun, of laughter! Every moment of the day we have the opportunity to be cheerful, let's make that choice today.

Choosing to be cheerful is liberating, it raises our vibration and acts as the catalyst for cheerfulness to spread around us.

When we are being cheerful, then laughter, joy and fun manifest in our lives as if by magic!

Have a cheerful day.

With love

x

117

*T*he beauty and power we have as humans manifests in our life with abundance once we have let go of all the fear our ego has created.

We hear of the fear of failure, the fear of success. The biggest fear that the ego creates for us is the fear of death.

Once we remember that there is nothing, absolutely nothing, to fear, then we find our true meaning in our heart and soul.

Live without fear, live with an open heart and be grateful. Then all fear melts away and a kind of serene certainty flows through us.

With love

x

*S*ee the beauty and feel the miracle of our daily lives. There is so much around us that demonstrates the wonder of the universe, yet we rarely take time to pause and acknowledge let alone appreciate it.

There are many reasons, many excuses, many stories that we incant every day as to why it's ok for us to lead our lives with blinkers on. Most people believe those excuses most of the time.

But now what's happening is that we humans are waking up. One by one the momentum is building. As we awaken, we recognise those excuses for what they really are: excuses of the ego.

Notice the stories you tell yourself. Recognise them as stories and then decide if those stories really serve you. Do they really enable you to live the life of your dreams?

As we begin to awaken we realise that whatever level we are playing at, it's way too small. We are capable of so much more and that so much more comes about when we connect with our heart and soul and the dreams that come from our heart and soul.

With love

x

119

*B*e grateful for and take care of your health. It's so easy to take good health for granted until we find we're no longer healthy.

The absence of pain and the vibrant energy of a curious child is our natural state. Any pain or disease is a sign of dis-ease.

Consider that for a moment: dis-ease. It means that we're no longer at ease. Dis-ease in our body is invariably an indication that somewhere our life is misaligned. That misalignment usually stems from us living in and listening to our head and therefore not following our heart.

Live well, feed yourself great nutrition, drink lots of water, listen to your heart and have fun along the way. That's a way of living that supports our body's requirements for good health and a vibrant life.

With love

x

120

Letting go can be a huge human challenge. We have a tendency to cling on to things such as life, childhood, partners, possessions.

True freedom and abundance flows freely when we let go. When we release not only the things we cling on to but we release our dreams and we release our expectations, then everything we truly desire manifests in our lives.

That manifestation is in the hands of the universe. We need to let go of details about where, when and particularly how. Let the universe do its work. Our role is to let go.

Free yourself. Let go

With love

X

121

*F*eel the flow of energy in your body. Pause and breathe and notice the energy.

As we pay attention to energy, after a while it becomes difficult to distinguish our human boundaries. Energetically we are all as one, all part of the energy on the planet.

This is where our human minds get challenged because our conscious minds tend to live within the human, physical world.

If we let go of the self-created limitations of the mind and allow our love to flow, then miracles occur, giant leaps in understanding and connection take place.

Feel the energy, feel the love.

With love

x

122

*O*ur imagination is so amazingly powerful that our brain has a tough job distinguishing between what we imagine and what we experience. Our ego knows this.

Many of the ego-created thoughts are brought to life through imagined experiences. That way the ego knows that our brain will be more likely to take these imagined experiences and believe them to be true.

Notice your thoughts, how vividly the mind runs those stories. They look and feel pretty realistic. Which is all fab when our thoughts are heart-based and therefore serving our best interests.

The thoughts that come from our ego are equally vivid and realistic but never serve our best interests.

Notice what goes through your mind today. Does it come from your heart or your ego? Will you pay attention to it or not? Your future depends on it.

With love

x

123

*C*onnecting with our heart and being grateful is the pathway to untold abundance and joy, not only for ourselves but also as a catalyst for those around us. Giving ourselves the gift of space and time is one way to accelerate that process.

Take a few minutes every day to meditate or to practice yoga or to listen to spiritual leaders, or whichever practice works best for you. The benefits cascade through to all areas of your life.

The greatest benefits are those of increased connection with yourself and a feeling of gratitude. Somehow taking those few minutes every day sends strong messages to our heart and soul, firstly that we acknowledge its very existence and secondly that we are listening to its wisdom and love.

Give yourself this beautiful gift. Notice how your life transforms in many ways at many levels. Watch as miracles occur.

With love

x

124

*L*iving in the moment, being present. We read and hear so much about being present, but what does it really mean?

The thing is that it's not something new that we need to learn. It's something we know that we need to remember.

When we are born and as young children, the only thing we know is the present; we live in the moment. Remember playing with your friends and not getting home in time for dinner? Or getting so engrossed in your favourite game that you missed the bus home?

We know what it means to be present, to live in the moment. As time goes by we seem to forget as we learn to do more "important" human-created things.

But what is really important? What really serves us and the planet best? Working an extra hour to please the boss or remembering to live in this moment and this moment and this moment... always the present moment?

The world needs more people to remember what we knew as children. Live in the moment.

With love

x

125

*L*ove your life, be an example to everyone, be an example of what it is to live your life with love! Start by loving yourself, as you are, right here, right now.

You are perfect. We are all perfect, just as we are. None of us need fixing, because we're not broken; we're perfect.

Our society bombards us with messages of how we can lose weight, change our appearance, wear different clothes to change how we look. The underlying implication is that there is something not quite right with us that needs to be fixed.

That's wrong! We do not need fixing; there is nothing broken.

Love yourself, love your life. Know that you are perfect in every moment of your life. Being perfect doesn't mean that you never change, it means that in this moment you are perfect and by acknowledging that perfection you are loving yourself for who you are. Once you love and acknowledge yourself then you are able to truly love and acknowledge others.

Love you, perfect you, every moment of every day.

With love

x

126

*T*here seems to be almost a fear of silence, of the space between activities and events. There is so much space-filling and silence-filling noise and distraction. But really, what is there to be fearful of?

The space and silence is where we are so often best able to connect with ourselves. Perhaps that is what people have become fearful of: being connected with the truth of who they are.

Yet, the truth of who we are is everything that we are here to live and to share. But the fear of that truth, the fear of the shining light that we are means that so much of our life is lived in the dark! Where's the sense, where's the passion, where's the love in that?

Revel in the silence, seek and enjoy the spaces in your life. For it is in those moments that you will truly be living.

With love

x

127

*T*aking some moments every day for ourselves might seem selfish, it might seem indulgent and it's almost certainly something we might squeeze in if we have time.

Whether it's meditation, yoga, a few moments in quiet reflection, a short walk for the purpose of creating space in your day, the important thing is to take some moments every day for ourselves.

It's not selfish or indulgent. In the same way that our body functions best with sufficient water and food, our connection with spirit is stronger when we acknowledge that we deserve time for ourselves.

There are many examples where 10-20 minutes of meditation a day has transformed lives. Perhaps start with a couple of minutes of silent reflection, paying attention to your breath and letting go of all thoughts. Notice how refreshing just those two minutes can be.

Take time for you. You're worth it.

With love

x

*W*e often choose to believe or are led to believe that the lives of others are better than our own, whether it be in terms of health, wealth, fitness, fame, relationships, lifestyle...

This raises a number of questions and challenges. Fundamentals first: What do you get from comparing yourself with others? We are here to live our own life and be true to ourselves, not to measure ourselves against others.

Secondly, what is the truth? We don't know the truth about anybody else's life. Let's stick with our truth, let's live our life by being the best version of us that we can be, in every moment of every day.

Live your life. You are amazing.

Leave comparisons to others.

And one final word: Others will be comparing themselves with you right now, and seeing aspects of your life that they are dreaming about for their own life...

With love

x

129

Make the most of every moment. Set goals, plan for the future, but don't live today on the basis that you'll feel happier when... Be happy now, in this moment, for it is our only moment.

So often we allow ourselves to be seduced by our ego into living in the future. With thoughts like *when we get that car* or *when our children are at school* or *when we move to the bigger house* or *when we take a vacation* or, or, or...

Why not be happy now? You can always be happy when you get a car, move to a bigger house, etc., etc., but be happy in this present moment. By being happy in this moment and this moment, we are being happy in the present, and if we are happy in each present moment, then guess what? Our whole lifetime is happy!

Be happy, right here, right now.

With love

X

130

*T*here is so much junk around that people allow to occupy their lives. There's emotional junk, physical junk, written junk, spoken junk, junk thoughts, all kinds of junk.

We deserve to live junk free. It is entirely our choice as to what junk we allow into our life. The thing is that every piece of junk we allow to occupy our life simply dulls our light.

We all have our light. And all our light wants to do is to shine brightly. For many of us, our light never gets to shine because of all the junk we allow to occupy our life.

Notice where you have junk in your life and start de-junking. Let go of the junk in your life. Every day let go of some junk and notice the changes that manifest in your being. You'll also notice how much lighter you feel as you let go of the weight of the junk.

Let your light shine bright.

With love

x

131

*O*ne of the greatest gifts we have to offer is to listen — to really listen so that whoever is speaking feels heard.

True listening only takes place when we are present. Therefore the gift is ours as well. We gift ourselves the beauty of being present.

Think about the conversations you've been involved with over the past few days. In how many of those conversations were you 100% present?

Many times our mind wanders onto some other subject: the shopping list, where we're going at the weekend, a bill we need to pay, etc., etc. We also have the distractions of social media, instant messages, emails...

How does it feel when you're saying something and the person you're talking with is looking at their phone, responding to messages, gazing into the distance? We notice when people are present and when they're not.

So give yourself and others the gift of being present and truly listening to what's being said. Listen from your heart and notice how the whole interaction transforms for both of you.

With love

x

We have so much we could be grateful for. The choice we make about being grateful is one that shapes the whole of our life.

We have the power to choose in every moment of every day whether we are going to be grateful about anything, about a few things, about a lot of things or about everything!

Imagine the difference in your life if you choose to be grateful about more things than you currently are.

For example, instead of enduring the journey to work, how about being grateful for your health being good enough to enable you to make that journey, being grateful for the transport that enables you to get to work, being grateful for the air that you breath, being grateful for the trees that not only contribute to air that you breath but also provide homes for birds and squirrels as well as visual beauty.

And so on and so on... There is so much to be grateful for at a time (the journey to work) when many people don't appear to be being grateful.

It really is a choice and it really is transformative.

Gratitude.

With love

x

133

*I*magine a life without boundaries, a life with limitless possibilities, where love is everywhere and miracles take place in every moment of every day.

Imagine a world that's been created as a play area purely for the purposes of having fun and enjoying life. A world where whatever our heart truly desires manifests.

Guess what? No need to imagine a life and a world like that, because that is the world we live in. As humans we have become very good at distracting ourselves from these truths and blocking the flow of energy that enables us to experience the world and our life in the way we can imagine it.

Allow the energy to flow, get out of your own way and notice what you notice. Life is so much simpler than we've been led to believe; enjoy the simplicity and magic of the world and this life.

With love

x

*L*ove the joy of life. Skip, dance, sing, laugh — whatever is joyful for you, do it some more.

When you're being love and doing whatever feels joyful to you, then your energy and light shine through, lighting the way for you and for others.

Live a joyful life.

With love

x

135

*G*ive thanks for your daily blessings and experiences. Appreciate the miracles all around you.

We can so easily take the blessings in our daily lives for granted. Sometimes doing something as simple as sharing part of our daily life with a friend enables us to experience it anew. As a consequence we are reminded that what we might consider an everyday event is a once in a lifetime experience for others.

Experience your day today as though for the first time. Notice what you notice. Feel the wonderment that brings.

We are all truly blessed, every day. Sometimes the miracles in our life are overlooked because they appear familiar. Enjoy the magic that every day brings.

With love

x

136

*F*eel the beauty and love of your heart. There are many opportunities every day when we might feel challenged. Often external events, the behaviour of others, life, death, war can distract us from the truth of beauty and love in our heart.

One of the many amazing things about human life is that we only ever have the moment that is with us now. And each moment is an opportunity to feel the beauty and love in our heart.

The more present we are in every moment of our life the more we feel that beauty and connection with the love in our heart.

Pause, breathe, notice your breath. Let your thoughts drift through, thank them for showing up and return to noticing your breath...

Be present.

With love

x

137

*P*ay attention to your intuition, listen to your heart. The wisdom we have available to us is beyond our comprehension.

How many times do we have some kind of feeling in our body when we're about to do something that doesn't feel quite right? Or maybe we sense that today we would be better served by doing something differently, even though we might have done it the same way many times before?

Trust those feelings, listen to those signs. We truly are guided, if only we allow it to be so.

Live from the heart of your soul.

With love

x

138

*T*he joy and magnificence of the sun rising is one of those daily miracles we can come to take for granted. Yet its beauty often defies description.

There are so many other aspects of the rising of the sun for which we can be grateful. It marks the dawning of a new day, it warms the air that we breathe, it's an element in nature's process of renewal and so much more.

This is true even on those days when the sun rises behind the clouds. We might not witness the rising of the sun but we still experience the beauty of its effects.

Notice these daily miracles. Being grateful for these miracles means that being grateful becomes a way of life, and there's pure magic in gratitude.

With love

X

139

*L*ife is so much simpler than most people believe. Our conditioning tells us that there are many things to do, achievements to be achieved, places to go, people to see.

The truth is that we are here to be the best version of ourselves. And there's an associated truth, which is that we are the only person that can be the best version of us!

Therefore, any comparison between who we are being and any external reference is futile. It is only we who can be the best version of us, so it can never matter what anyone else thinks or says about who we are. It is our journey and our path to every day be the best version of us that we can be.

Just consider that for a few moments. It's not important where you live, what position you reach in business or society, whether you have a lifelong partner, what car you drive, etc., etc. The only thing that matters is that today you are being the very best version of you.

The only thing that matters is that today you are being the very best version of you.

With love

x

*T*he world is crying out for more people to shine their light, to connect with their soul, to be love. And it's something we all have within us.

It's up to each and every one of us to shine our own light. Shining our light is about clearing away the clutter that we've accumulated through our lives, the clutter that covers over the light we all have within us.

Release the clutter in your life, one piece at a time, one object at a time, one thought at a time, one emotion at a time. Day by day through releasing the acquired clutter, step by step our light is able to shine through.

Enable your light to shine. You deserve it, we all deserve it, and the world needs more lights to shine.

With love

x

141

Notice today how often you are judging the behaviour and actions of yourself and others. In particular, the judgements we make of ourselves are often harsh and rarely uplifting.

Rather than judging behaviours and actions, let go of the judgements and accept those behaviours and actions as they are: the best that we can do and be, based on all that we know.

Judgement usually involves some kind of comparison with something or someone external. Yet, the only thing that truly matters is that we are being the best version of us that we can be. The best version of us is always doing and being the best that we can in that moment.

Give yourself and everyone else a break. Quit judging and be accepting. In acceptance there is peace, gratitude and love. Doesn't that feel like a beautiful place to be?

Acceptance of yourself and everyone else is a gift that is freely available to all of us. Let's share that gift.

With love

x

142

*E*very experience, every interaction is a gift, a gift for everyone involved.

Sometimes the gift takes a while to appear. Sometimes the gift is not readily recognisable as a gift.

Believe that there is always a gift and be grateful. Belief and gratitude will enable the gifts to be revealed.

Keep bringing yourself as you are to experience every moment. We are all essential to the co-creative experience of life. We all bring our own gifts to every experience.

Enjoy your gifts, receive gratefully and give with love.

With love

x

143

*A*s humans, we tend to be outcome focused, whether it be on grades in school, completion of projects, achieving targets, etc.

What we are remembering is that the joy of life is not in the outcome. The joy of life is in the process that leads to an outcome.

Our lives would be so much more joyous if we let go of outcome and simply decided to be love, to be grateful. And from that place of love and gratitude, we do good things that bring joy to us and the world. We still get an outcome: the outcome is joy!

Let go of any specific outcome. Be love, be gratitude. There will still be outcomes. Notice how those outcomes serve you and those around you and those around them...

With love

x

144

*T*he ripple effects of our ways of being and the actions that follow continue way beyond that which is apparent to us.

So, continue being loving and grateful; you deserve to be that way

Every so often we'll notice the ripple effect of our ways of being. Someone might tell us something they've noticed in us that has inspired them, or we might read something and recognise our influence on the person who wrote it.

On those occasions, just imagine for a moment all the people and activities that our ripples have reached. Our conscious being is aware of the range of our ripples. But as humans, we tend to rely on direct feedback from other humans.

Trust that by being loving and grateful, not only is your life enhanced but there are literally millions of lives that benefit as your ripples spread and spread and spread.

With love

x

145

*E*verybody is being the best version of themselves given what they know. When we know different, we are able to be different.

Sometimes we can find ourselves looking towards the behaviour of others with a feeling that maybe they should know better. Firstly, remember that we are all doing our best based on what we know.

In addition, the universe is such an amazing place, it presents the perfect situations and opportunities for us to learn whatever we need to learn whenever the time is right.

Imagine the world as a mirror. What we observe in others is in some way a reflection of us. Therefore if we see something in others that we feel could be changed, let's look into ourselves and see what there is for us to learn in that moment.

Rejoice in the joy of the universe, the amazing gifts we receive each and every day. Be loving, be grateful, be open to receive the gifts of the universe.

With love

x

146

*F*or much of our lives we are interacting with others, we are involved in relationships of many types: the brief relationship with the checkout assistant in a store, an intimate relationship with our partner, relationships with work colleagues, the relationship with ourselves, family relationships, etc., etc.

Nurture all your relationships, however fleeting those relationships might be. Every interaction is enhanced when a relationship is based on love. Every interaction is enhanced when we are present in each moment and we accept another person exactly as they are in that moment.

It can happen that we show up in a relationship with a pile of baggage, memories, stories, emotions from a previous exchange or relationship, etc. When we are truly present in each and every moment, then none of that "stuff" contaminates the pure beauty of the present moment.

What's more, all our relationships (beginning with the relationship with ourself) are enhanced beyond measure. We'll have interactions with others that will be of a quality that is extraordinary!

Being present... the "secret" to beautiful relationships.

With love

x

147

*B*eing grateful for all that our life holds might not always feel easy. From time to time (always at the perfect moment) we are offered reminders of aspects of our life which maybe we haven't been being as grateful for as much as we might.

Be grateful for those reminders as well as the people, events, circumstances that brought them into your life. We can also be grateful that we're noticing those reminders, that our senses are open and alive to receive them.

As we practise being grateful we remember to be grateful just for being alive and for the miracle that it is to be human. Then gratitude becomes habitual, which is a beautiful place to be.

With love

x

148

*S*ometimes do you feel like there's a scream or yelp or groan that's building up inside of you? It's the voice of your heart, grabbing your attention as it calls out.

Our heart is strong and holds much wisdom. Our heart knows that when we live in our heart then our life experience is enhanced to levels that our mind (ego) cannot conceive.

The conditioning of our human world has been unconsciously based on the will of our mind being superior to the love of our heart. Increasingly we're waking up to the truth, which is that it is from our heart that we are truly creative.

What's more, we are all truly creative when we are being love, the love of our heart.

Love yourself.

Love humanity.

Lead the way.

Live from the love of your heart.

With love

x

149

*L*etting yourself go, being vulnerable — what feelings does that bring up for you? We tend to be educated to protect ourselves and keep ourselves in control.

The truth is that it's only by being vulnerable that we are really living our life, living as our authentic, creative self.

We have been led to believe that being vulnerable is risky, that it puts us at risk. The real risk in life is that by not enabling ourselves to be vulnerable we live an existence rather than live a life.

Which feels more compelling and fulfilling to you, an existence or a life?

You choose: being vulnerable and living or... not.

With love

x

150

*T*ake a few moments today to consider how connected you feel with yourself and with everyone and everything around you.

Energetically we are all as one, connected every moment of every day.

Any disconnection originates in our mind. It is caused by our ego. All conflict at any level has its origins in the mind and ego of humans; it does not reflect the energetic connectedness that is the real truth.

As we are all connected energetically, what does it mean then when a group of humans declares war on another group of humans? We are at war with ourselves. We are attacking, torturing and killing ourselves.

Enjoy the beauty of connectedness, and before engaging in conflict remember that all conflict is really conflict with ourselves.

With love

x

151

*E*njoy the challenges of your day, of your life. Without challenges we would not experience the personal growth that enables our life purpose to manifest.

It doesn't always feel that way, and challenges often feel like they arrive at the worst possible time. In truth, challenges always arrive at the perfect moment for us to remember whatever it is we are meant to remember at that precise moment on our soul's journey.

Best of all is to be grateful for the challenges, to give thanks and to fully embrace those challenges in that moment.

Enjoy your challenges. Discover your life purpose.

With love

x

152

*T*he beauty of our human life is often brought to the forefront of our hearts by the contrast that life presents to us. We are all seeking the light, the light of life that shines so bright.

How do we recognise the light? It's certainly a feeling of connection and oneness. A feeling of physical lightness as well as spiritual light.

Consider the contrast to light. Dark is the contrast to light and it is through knowing and experiencing the dark that we can recognise the light.

Yet the dark feels dark, it feels uncomfortable. Invariably, when experiencing dark we seek to quickly move away from the dark.

Take care and give yourself the gift of time to truly understand what a particular dark experience is bringing to you. When we don't take the time to truly understand what the dark is bringing, then we will return to a deeper dark place at a later date.

Enjoy and be grateful for every experience of the dark. Relish the experience with your heart for it is through these dark experiences that we appreciate and truly enjoy our light.

With love

x

153

*C*ommit to being a lifelong learner. As humans, we are either growing or dying. This applies to every aspect of our being. If we are not learning, then we are un-learning.

Learning is always more fun when we are passionate about the subject. Most of us don't find our passion before we commit to lifelong learning.

Often one of the first steps to uncovering our passion is the commitment to be a lifelong learner. The greater our commitment to learning, the more likely we are to uncover our passion and to live our passion in this lifetime.

Learning is often associated with education, which takes many of us back to our school days. Learning and school life are not the same thing; please do not confuse the two. It is possible to learn at school, just as it is possible to learn outside of school.

Once we commit to learning, there are opportunities to learn in every moment of every day!

Keep on learning!

With love

x

154

*W*hat does feeling content mean to you? How content do you feel about yourself and your life?

Whilst considering those questions, be careful to distinguish between contentment and comfort. Feeling comfortable and feeling content are two very different things.

There is a saying that "comfort is a killer". Comfort usually means that we are living a life that feels comfortable, which doesn't involve anything outside of our comfort zone. This is an environment of stagnation.

Contentment is very different. Contentment is about a feeling of peace and connection. When feeling content we are readily able to live in the moment, without regrets about the past or fears about the future. We are content.

Now consider contentment, what it means to you and how content you are feeling.

With love

X

155

*L*ooking around, it's possible to conclude that life is a serious experience that doesn't involve a whole lot of joy and definitely not too much smiling! The truth is that life is as joyous as we decide it is going to be.

As humans we are blessed with the ability to choose the meaning that we attach to every moment of our life. Recognising this choice, what will you choose?

Remembering that each moment only comes around once, why not choose to embrace every moment and express yourself with joy and love?

Collectively we co-create our human experience. We choose how we contribute to that human experience.

Let's choose love, gratitude, and joy.

With love

x

156

*T*ake a step towards your heartfelt passion. Take a step every day and your life experience transforms. Be assured that for most of the journey no one is certain of the nature of their heartfelt passion, so please don't use that uncertainty as an excuse for not taking a step.

Start by taking a step every day. Tiny steps are more than enough. A small step every day will naturally transform into a giant leap before you know it.

Whilst we often believe that the journey to our heartfelt passion is a series of steps and leaps, in truth it is a matter of step by step removing the worldly clutter that over time has obscured our heartfelt passion.

Our heartfelt passion is within us. We all have a heartfelt passion, so we can be certain that the "prize" exists; and what's more, it's yearning to be uncovered.

What you'll notice along the way is that the journey of rediscovery is in itself simply awesome.

Take a step today, and tomorrow and every day. Enjoy the process.

With love

x

157

*B*e bold!

We inhabit a world where there is so much emphasis on expectation management, so much conditioning, so much being realistic. None of these are in any way about shooting for the stars or being bold, they are all in some way about dampening down, dumbing down our human experience.

There are many culturally accepted excuses for not being bold: the bills to pay, our children, our partner, our friends, our family, our job, our career, our studies, etc., etc., etc. — all familiar excuses for not being bold.

The world needs more boldness, for more people to come alive and truly live. Look at your excuses for not being bold and recognise that those excuses are simply that: excuses.

Be bold!

With love

x

158

*G*ift yourself and those you interact with the gift of being fully present.

So often we find ourselves in a conversation where most of our attention is on what we are going to say next and we barely register what the other person is saying, let alone notice their non-verbal messages. This is not being present or living in the moment.

In fact we are often paying more attention to the conversation in our head, our internal dialogue, than we are to the person who believes they're having a conversation with us!

How does it feel when you have a conversation with someone who is not fully present? Do you feel heard? Do you feel that they're fully engaged? Or are you so not present that you don't even notice?

This moment is the only moment we have. Being fully present in this moment immeasurably enhances the quality of our being. What's more, it's a gift to those we interact with, because they feel our presence. They might not know what it is, but they will feel something special about interactions with us. They will feel seen and heard in a way that doesn't typically happen.

Today, have at least one conversation where you are truly present, with no distractions, paying attention to both the verbal and nonverbal communication. Notice how that feels

With Love

for you, and know that it is a gift for whoever you are in conversation with.

With love

x

159

*T*ake a moment, at least one moment every day to connect with your heart. Feel the beat of your physical heart and recognise that organ as a metaphor for your heart, what is truly at the heart of you.

What is at the heart of you is not physical; it is the essence of you in this lifetime.

Connecting with your own heart opens up limitless possibilities to connect with the hearts of those around you. As humans, heartfelt connection with another is one of the experiences in our life that lifts our love and vibration.

Take a moment to feel your physical heart, feel the beating of your heart. Notice the emotions that that brings up for you. Embrace those emotions and sit with those emotions.

Your heart knows. Connect with your heart. Listen to your heart.

With love

X

160

*T*hree L's to embrace and have in your life on a daily basis: live, laugh and love. Three L's, short, simple words, but so powerful for us and our quality of life.

When we can look back at the end of the day and know in ourselves that we have lived, we've laughed and we've loved, then it's likely that our day has been fab for us and for those we've interacted with.

Today, as you go through your day, notice how it feels when you're living (in the moment as opposed to existing in the past or future). Notice how it feels when you're laughing, and notice how it feels when you're being loving (always starting by being loving of yourself). Notice how you feel and notice how the quality of your interactions changes.

Live, laugh and love.

With love

x

161

*T*ake time today to connect with a loved one, let them know that you are there, that you care for them and that you love them.

Always be sure to connect with yourself and let you know that you love you, for without loving ourselves we are not able to truly love another.

We can share our love in so many ways. It's not only about telling people we love them, or sending flowers, or romantic dates. Simply coming home early from work to create time for each other, or a random phone call to let them know you're there, or a warm hug, etc., etc.

The world could do with more people sharing love and being loving.

We are blessed to be able to be love, it's a gift. When we are being love, our world somehow magically transforms, as does the world of those we come into contact with.

With love

x

162

We hear and read about values and beliefs. About how important it is to know our values, to determine what we value most and what we value least.

Why?

What are values? Values are whatever feelings we determine are most important in our life. Values are things like love, gratitude, health, compassion, security, adventure, etc.

The thing is, usually we don't decide what we want to value. We learn what to value from our parents, our family, our teachers, our peers, our friends, society's expectations.

There are many inputs into what become our values, yet the one obvious missing input is us. What is it that we want to value that will best serve us?

As is so often the case, our heart has the answer. Tuning into and listening to our heart will enable us to connect with whatever we value most.

Take a few moments to tune into the beat, the vibration of your heart and notice what comes up for you. Let that be the beginning of you creating your own, personal values for your life. After all, it is your life; you might as well design it so that it works for you!

With love

x

Tim Brister

*L*ove the joy of life, the simple joys we experience every day. It's common to get bogged down and distracted by the noise and clutter that can mask the joy of life. But remember to choose your way for yourself.

The really bizarre thing is that the noise and clutter is rarely ours! There is no shortage of available noise and clutter. The question for us is, how much of the available noise and clutter do we let into our life?

It's our choice whether to be grateful for the joys of life, to enable those joys to flow freely into and through our life.

Alternatively we can choose to be overtaken by the noise and clutter created by others and allow their noise and clutter to flow freely through our life.

Which would you choose? Which do you choose? Which will you choose?

Choose wisely and joyfully with abundance and gratitude.

With love

x

164

*R*emember your reason for being, the light that shines within you. That remembering is what transforms our experience on earth and the experience of those we interact with.

When we live in alignment with our reason for being, our light shines bright for us and everyone around us. The magic is that it really is simply a case of remembering, because when we are born, we know why we are born, we know our reason for being.

As we go through life we never lose our reason for being. We might forget it, we might lose sight of it from time to time but it always dwells within us.

The first segment of our life is all about remembering our reason for being. Then, the second segment of our life is about living in alignment with that reason for being and truly living our life!

The more people who are living their life in alignment with their reason for being, the more light that is shining in the world to light the way for others to remember their reason for being. Let's live our life with our light shining bright, for us and for all those who will see our light and use it to help them remember their way.

The experience of meeting someone whose light is shining is truly inspirational. Imagine how you'll feel when it is your light that is shining!

With love

x

165

*B*eing present in this moment is completely transformational. The quality of your relationships with yourself and others will simply explode.

But beware the resourcefulness of the ego. The ego fears the present and so will do whatever it takes to keep us out of the present moment.

One of the ego's favourite tricks is to let us believe that we are fully present in the moment and then to sneak in distractions which slowly and subtly take us away from the moment whilst still giving us the belief that we are 100% present.

Check in with yourself regularly; take a breath and sit in silence to re-connect with yourself in the present moment.

The ego will fight to the death. It is resourceful but it cannot withstand the presence of being in the moment.

Live in the moment. Connect fully with yourself and the world around you.

With love

x

166

*L*isten to what makes your heart sing, follow the whims of your heart and live a life of passion. You deserve it and the world needs more people to live a life of passion.

We are conditioned to acquire skills and knowledge, to further our education, to settle down. There is nothing wrong with any of those things. We can choose the extent to which we do all of them.

However, for us to live a life that fulfils our heart, we first of all need to feel and act on what our heart is telling us and to listen to our heart, for our heart knows what lights us up and why it lights us up.

Be aware; our heart will not tell us how to get what we want.

When we truly feel and believe what we want and why we want it, then how we get there will come to us so long as we keep believing.

Listen to your heart, create the life of your dreams and light up the world.

With love

x

*A*s humans our ability to completely change our life in a heartbeat is quite remarkable and massively underutilised. When we feel anything less than outstanding it feels grim, and very often it feels like there's no end to that feeling.

Yet we can turn that around in a moment. In any given moment we can choose to change what we focus on, change the way we are talking (to ourselves) or change how we're using our body (e.g., sit up straight instead of slouching, walk with purpose instead of dawdling, move vigorously instead of not moving, breath deeply, etc.).

When we really understand and believe that it is we who determine how we feel, then our opportunities to feel outstanding explode. In fact, we can feel outstanding any moment we choose to!

It might seem hard to believe but language is absolutely the easiest way to condition yourself to feel outstanding, because every day, numerous times a day we'll be asked how we're feeling. The most common response is "ok" or "good" or "getting by" or something similar. Those responses are conditioning us to feel that way!

Why not condition yourself to feel better than that? When you're asked how you feel, don't sink to the level of the masses, shine your light, lead the way and choose to feel outstanding. Try it today, see how it feels. You'll get some strange looks but notice how you feel.

Tell yourself and the world that you are outstanding. Because you are!

With love

x

168

*I*f ever you feel unclear or uncertain about what to do in any circumstance, take a breath, feel what is in your heart and decide how to be. From that place of heartfelt being, whatever you do will be the right thing.

It's far more important that we decide how to be and then do, rather than deciding what to do.

Of course we do things; we are humans and we do stuff. But, it's not the things we do that make the biggest difference; it's the way we are being (whilst we are doing) that makes the biggest difference.

Our way of being is the context from which we are living life from moment to moment. Therefore it shapes everything we are doing in that moment.

Our way of being is always found in the wisdom of our heart; we just need to give ourselves the gift of listening to the wisdom in our heart.

Imagine the difference if you are being grateful as opposed to being angry or being jealous. Imagine how whatever you do would be affected by those different ways of being.

With love

x

169

*K*nowing and trusting that everything is unfolding for us in divine order completely changes our whole life experience. As difficult as it might be to believe in some moments, it is true that everything is happening in divine order.

This does not mean we should stop taking action or stop being proactive because everything is going to happen anyway.

What it means is that everything is happening in divine order as it is meant to happen as we co-create each moment of our lives.

The divine perfection is found in the way our lives unfold. For example, we are challenged by exactly the right thing at exactly the right time to enable us to remember what we need to remember. This does not mean that we necessarily understand in that moment what there is for us in that moment; we simply need to trust that everything is unfolding in divine order.

Once we do truly believe that everything is unfolding in divine order it takes away a lot of stress from life. We realise that all we need to be is present in the present moment and do whatever feels right from that presence in that moment.

Trust.

With love

x

Tim Brister

170

*C*onnecting with the simple pleasures and joys of life not only brings a smile to our heart but enables us to be more grounded. Keeping connected with nature, with ourselves, with our heart somehow maintains and develops our feeling of certainty that we as humans are living our human life in a way that feels good and true to us.

What a true life is for each of us is individual to each of us. There is no ideal or perfect or "right" way to live. Only you know the way that feels good and true to you.

What is true is that the more each of us stays grounded and reconnects with nature, with ourselves and with love, then that knowing of what feels good and true to us becomes clearer and is more frequently in our awareness.

Live the life that feels good and true to you.

Live your life!

With love

x

171

*T*he beauty of true friendship is a gift that's all too easy to overlook or take for granted. Yet the value of true friendship is a treasure beyond measure.

True friends are always there for us, never judging us, never conditional with their friendship and their support of us. True friends love and accept us in a way that others don't.

The strange thing is to wonder how it is we are drawn to our true friends. It looks like a mystical, miraculous set of circumstances and happenings that brings us together.

Consider this: perhaps there is no mysticism to it; it's not a miracle; it's simply two souls coming together, knowing that in this lifetime they are friends that are meant to come together to support each other through this human experience.

Whatever you believe about the way in which our true friendships come about, nurture your friendships, love and accept your friends.

With love

x

172

*L*oving ourselves and feeling our heart — not the physical beat of our heart (though that is a beautiful thing too!) — feeling the essence of our heart, the love that is in our heart. The more of us that connect with ourselves, feel our heart's essence and feel comfortable loving ourselves, the more the vibration of the world is raised and the more love and abundance we all feel.

The first step is to truly love ourselves, to feel comfortable loving ourselves recognising that we can feel love whenever we choose, because at our essence we are love; it's just that life comes along and our true essence can get obscured.

Knowing that our true essence is love and being connected to our true essence means that we will be radiating love in every moment. And we will never know the extent to which our radiating love impacts on the rest of the planet.

Our radiating love could touch any number of the people we connect with on a daily basis. They might not be aware that our radiating love has touched them, but they in turn will connect with others in a way which reflects radiating love and so on and so on...

That's how being in touch with our true essence and radiating love contributes towards raising the vibration of the planet.

With love

X

173

*B*eing grateful in every moment will transform your life. When you're being grateful you will inevitably feel love because gratitude is a way of being that comes from our heart.

The sure thing about life is that there's always something to be grateful about. If it's the singing of the birds, the sun in the sky, the beating of our heart, the roof over our head, there are so many things that we could be grateful for.

Even in what might feel like dark or challenging moments, there is a reason to be grateful.

Practice being grateful today. Take a moment to notice ten things you can be grateful for in that moment.

Take a moment like that and be grateful more than once a day.

Soon you'll want to be consciously grateful all the time because it feels so good, it takes your attention to parts of your life that you're grateful for, and because when we are grateful, the universe presents more for us to be grateful for.

With love

x

174

*A*s humans, from a young age we are typically conditioned to form our own views and judgements of people, events, experiences, objects, etc., etc. As we develop into adults we tend to develop the habit of judging people, starting with ourselves.

Take a moment to recall the ways in which you've judged yourself over the past few days. When you've been judging yourself, has that been a positive or a negative experience? Did you judge yourself as having done well or did your judgement lead to a feeling that you could (should) have done better?

In the main, when we judge ourselves, we tend to take the opportunity to give ourselves a bit of a beating up and dwell on all the things we could have done better. Rarely do we judge ourselves as having been outstandingly successful.

Similarly when we judge others, we tend to take the opportunity to focus on what we perceive as areas of fault/weakness, unless we're really judging ourselves, in which case we dwell on the strengths of others in order to accentuate our perceived weaknesses!

For the next 48 hours, suspend all judgement. Accept yourself and others. Accept that everyone is doing the best they can based on everything they know and they've experienced in their life to date.

Notice how things change for you, notice how much kinder it feels to not be judging. Then, if it feels good, carry on suspending judgement.

With love

x

175

*R*emembering the purpose for your life might feel like something huge that we could struggle with for many, many years. The simple truth is that we are born knowing our purpose.

We are born knowing our purpose. We are born knowing that our human existence vibrates with joy, love and passion when we are living our purpose.

We can be led to believe that our purpose is some huge accomplishment that sits outside of us.

The truth is that our purpose is within us. Our soul always knows the purpose of this human experience. The challenge for us humans is to get our humanness out of the way and enable the joy of living in alignment with our purpose to shine through.

The way to connect and live in alignment with our purpose is to live from our heart, to be love and create the clear space for our purpose to shine through.

The daily practice of living from our heart will inevitably lead to our purpose manifesting in our life, and then there is no need to struggle in any way; just clear the way for the purpose that is inside of us to shine through.

With love

x

*S*ometimes we are faced with a decision, and we look at all the options; we look at the pro's and the con's, we might even do some form of cost benefit analysis, and yet we still feel unsure as to what to do.

We can also remember a time when we were faced with a decision and we instinctively decided. We followed our gut instinct and that was enough for us to decide.

If we allow ourselves to listen to our instinct, intuitively we know what do in any situation. We need to give our instinct the space to come through, take away all the considerations of the mind.

Then just trust.

The mind does not want to believe that instinct can be as powerful as it truly is. Give your mind a break and enable your instinct to come through.

With love

x

177

Never underestimate the power of a smile to a stranger, or the impact of simply listening to a friend who needs to be heard, or the effect of some encouragement offered to a child. Being compassionate and thoughtful and supportive has effects far beyond those that we might see or feel.

Think of experiences in your life that you treasure. Then step back through the series of events, decisions, interactions, connections, support that you had along the way to reach that experience.

At each of those points along the way it's highly unlikely that you (or those involved in those points along the way) could have imagined the experiences that lay ahead. Those smiles, moments of attention, words of encouragement all contributed to you enjoying that treasured experience.

Be compassionate, caring, and loving to yourself and others. None of us ever know where that compassion and love could lead to!

With love

x

178

*O*ur human existence is such a blessing and it feels like it flashes by in the blink of an eye.

For those reasons (and maybe many others) decide to be the best version of you that you can be and to enjoy being the best version of you.

Accept that the best version of you changes and evolves as you remember more of what you're here to remember. Rejoice in being the current best version of you and commit to enjoy being the best version of you.

With love in your heart and joy in your step make the most of life's every moment!

With love

x

179

One of the greatest gifts we can share is that of connection. Being connected with ourselves is a beautiful gift for us. Connecting with others is like dropping a pebble in a pond, and the ripples spread way beyond those that we see.

Sometimes we forget that it's the small things that make such a difference. Taking time out to connect and converse with someone is one of those simple, small things that can completely transform someone's day.

Take a moment today to notice those around you who you can simply and easily connect with. Maybe a shop assistant, a bus driver, a work colleague, a homeless person.

In fact, how about, the next homeless person you see, simply talk with them, be truly present with them. Notice what happens for them and for you.

Invariably the gift of connection feels far more valuable to that person than whatever coins they receive.

The gift of connection.

With love

x

180

*A*t our heart we are love, we are loving souls co-creating a human experience. There is so much joy to be enjoyed and so much joy to be shared simply through being love.

If every one of us were to be loving every day, then the feeling of love in the world would increase exponentially. That's because the wide consequences of being loving cannot be imagined by the person who is loving.

Love really is contagious. Notice the energy when two loving beings connect. The love and energy around them radiates and reaches many, many others.

In turn those others whom the radiating love reaches then carry that loving radiance and energy with them. But even more, as well as carrying that loving radiance, their own loving radiance develops and expands, enabling many, many more people to be reached and feel loving.

And so on and so on.

Being love is an amazing place to be. Sharing that love is where the magic begins because then love's contagiousness is released to work its magic across the globe.

With love

x

181

Many times we are encouraged to reach out, to achieve recognition, to make it to the next level.

None of those are in themselves bad. However, there is often an accompanying message that we need to achieve something in order for us to be whole, to be our true selves. This message is flawed on many levels.

We arrive in this lifetime complete and whole. We do not need to achieve anything to be complete and whole.

Once we remember that we are complete, then the achievement of goals, targets, etc., flows freely and abundantly through us. But we do not need to achieve any of those things to be complete.

Not only does the message about needing to achieve to be complete reinforce the false message that we are not already complete, it also encourages us to look outside of ourselves for recognition and acknowledgement.

Looking outside ourselves for acknowledgement puts an element of our sense of well-being in the hands of others, when in truth it is entirely our choice how we choose to feel and be in any given moment.

Take ownership of your own well-being! Know that you are complete and watch the abundance of the universe flow in your life.

With Love

Choose your own way of being and feeling, moment by moment, day by day.

With love

x

182

*T*he joy, curiosity and adventure of childhood does not have to end or become curtailed because we reach a certain age, or job, or partner, or house, or car, or... anything.

Yet somehow by the time we reach adulthood, that curiosity, joy and adventure has disappeared, or at best makes only fleeting appearances in what becomes an otherwise mundane existence.

Just now, take a moment, clear your mind and ask your heart where the passion lies for you. Is it in the mundane or is it in joy, adventure and curiosity? Which makes your heart sing, your spirit leap, your step turn into a skip?

Rather than reflect on how life became mundane, decide today to be curious, to be adventurous, to be joyful. Rekindle your spirit, have a skip in your step.

With love

x

183

The never-ending abundance of miracles that are available for us to experience on a daily basis could provide a source for us to be grateful in every moment of every day. And there is a lot of gratitude around. However, there is also a lot of expectation, hate, anger and fear, none of which exist when we are being gratitude.

Is it possible that fear is at the core of these feelings? Is it possible that fear is the feeling that drives behaviours that are incompatible with gratitude and love?

When we are fearful, we focus on scarcity rather than abundance, we focus on hate rather than love, we focus on judgement rather than acceptance. When we are grateful our focus is on abundance, love, acceptance.

Notice where your attention is drawn.

Is it drawn towards judgement or acceptance? When we are drawn towards judgement, we are living in fear, we are not paying attention to the miracles all around us, we are living in scarcity.

Decide where you want to live. Do you want to be fearful or grateful?

Choose, with love

x

184

When we're young we all have dreams, we all imagine what our life will be like when we're grown up. How close is your life now to the life that you imagined when you were dreaming as a child?

For many people, the answer is that adult life is very different to the life that they imagined as a child. And for most of those people, adult life has less adventure, less excitement, less fun. It has more work, more bills, more stress.

What happens then between those childhood dreams and adult existence?

Most of us get caught up, we get caught up making other people's dreams come true, we get caught up making a living instead of living our dreams.

Many of us don't believe that we deserve to live the life of our dreams.

Whereas, really, the life of our dreams is the life we designed when we were young, free and connected with ourselves, before we let life distract us and before we allowed ourselves to believe that we didn't deserve our dream life.

The life we dreamt of as children is the life our heart desires. Why would we want to deny the desires of our heart?

Live your dreams — you deserve to!

With love

x

185

*T*he beauty in feeling connected with yourself, feeling your heart, your soul connecting is a joy to behold. Yet the levels of disconnection demonstrated every day by the vast majority of people is both astonishing and disturbing at the same time.

With disconnection comes the inability to be present, to truly be alive, because we only ever have this moment, and if we're not present to live in this moment, then moment by moment our life disappears without being lived. How does that feel?

It feels like one of the great misconceptions of the developed world is that the more technology we have to contact people, the more connected we are. Not so!

The first person for us to connect with is ourselves, which requires zero technology.

Once we have really connected with ourselves, then we will be able to be present for ourselves and others. Generally speaking, technology provides multiple ways for us to be distracted and non-present.

Be sure to control the way technology shows up in your life. There are amazing technological gifts, but we need to remember to act as the master of technology and not have technology be our master.

Something to think about.

With love

x

186

Many of us are so caught up in our own stuff, handling our life situation, that we lose sight of the value we can add, the contribution we can make beyond ourselves. Yet contributing beyond ourselves is one of those miraculous things that adds value to others but also has a payback for us that is amazing and invariably unexpected.

There are so many ways in which we can contribute beyond ourselves which don't have to be grand acts of contribution. Start by being loving to those you interact with. Listen, properly listen to others and when in conversation be present, put down the phone and really listen. Smile, with genuine love.

Here's something to think about. The simplest way to become a habitual contributor is to be grateful for all that you have in your life. By being grateful for what we have we become more open to contributing beyond ourselves.

Being grateful enables us to be more present, more connected, more loving. Being grateful deepens the level of connection with ourselves, and when we're deeply connected to ourselves we contribute with an ease and a flow that feels completely natural.

It might not seem obvious but it's really true. Being grateful will enable us to contribute more beyond ourselves.

With love

x

187

*B*ringing the best version of you to each moment of each day brings us such a feeling of inner calm, strength, connectedness, certainty and much more. There are also many benefits and consequences for others, but the benefits to us are magnificent and no more than each of us deserves.

How often do you qualify or put rules around when or if the best version of you is going to show up? We've all done it, saying that we'll really go for it once we have completed our work or got a new car or cleaned the house or had a coffee or, or, or.

WHY?

We are compromising our life for each and every moment that we withhold our best version of ourself from showing up! We know that the only moment we have is the present moment, so why would we want to live anything other than the best life we can live?

Give yourself permission to be the best version of you. Every moment of every day. You deserve it and so does the rest of the world.

With love

x

188

*D*emonstrating to you that you value you and that you love you is so important to your sense of self worth. Our sense of the worth of ourself reflects out on our world and our interactions in the world.

Our heart knows our truth. It knows how we feel about ourselves and the extent to which we value ourselves.

As humans, we generally like to appear confident, certain and sure of ourselves. And that might fool some other humans (it will never fool anyone else who is connected with themselves!) some of the time, but it will never fool your heart.

Putting on a show, living behind a facade are recipes for a life of dissatisfaction and misery. The misalignment that our heart feels at this facade means that at our core we are disconnected, we are not loving ourselves.

This results in a sad, slow death. Moment by moment, day by day, week by week our life force slips away beneath a web of lies. The most hurtful kind of lies, lies that we repeatedly tell ourself.

Remember that our heart knows our truth, our heart cannot be fooled.

Live your truth, whatever that is for you, moment to moment. Live your truth and your heart will sing with joy at the alignment of you!

With love

x

189

*T*he power of our intentions is boundless; never underestimate the power of your intentions. Once we remember that power and align our intentions with our soul, then we are in the flow of our human existence.

It is in the flow of our human existence that we find true joy. It's where our love flows, where our spirit soars, where our zest for life is abundant. Surely this feels like the place you'd want to be?

How is it that we're not all living in this beautiful place? We are good people, doing good things, so what's stopping us?

So often, what's stopping us, what's holding us back is a tiny, tiny misalignment. We haven't fully connected with our heart because our mind is still involved. The complete alignment of our intentions with our heart only comes once we have fully reconnected with our heart.

Let your heart direct your mind, let your heart quieten your mind so that you can reconnect with your heart. Then you are on the way to that flow state in which your intentions can align with your soul.

With love

x

*T*he abundance of the universe truly is unlimited. We put our own boundaries, rules, limits around ourselves and our lives. The universe will support us abundantly if we allow ourselves to be open to it.

So why do the vast majority of people decline the unlimited abundance of the universe and continue to limit their lives? One word: fear.

Many people are so wrapped up in the illusion of fear that they are not only fearful of failure they are fearful of success too! That's a sure way to feed the fear that keeps people away from the abundance of the universe.

Once we remember that fear is completely made up, it's an illusion created by humans, then we know that fear cannot have a hold over our thoughts, feelings or actions.

Stop living in the illusion of fear and enjoy the abundance of the universe. You deserve it.

With love

x

191

*T*ake some moments to just be. We live in a developed world where doing and achieving tend to be recognised. For all of our sakes, it's time to redress the balance and to be.

Being is not indulgent, it's not lazy, it's not self-centred.

The truth is that we are all being, all of the time. The trouble is that we are so busy doing that we tend to forget that if we chose to be and THEN do, our life would be more connected and fulfilling.

Giving ourselves the gift of just being is beneficial to us in so many ways. Just being tends to quieten the chatter in our minds. It also shows us what it is to be, something that has tended to become submerged under the constant doingness in the world today.

Love yourself, love others, lead the way. Choose to be.

With love

x

*B*eing grateful for what is. It sounds simple, but we often make it more difficult than it needs to be.

The beating of our heart, the rising of the sun, the oxygen that we breathe: all of these we could be grateful for every day.

There is a relationship between gratitude, love and abundance. The more we express our love, the more gratitude we feel. The more gratitude we feel, the more we express our love. The more grateful and loving we are, the more abundance comes into and through our life.

How awesome is that? The universe really is set up for abundance. When we are being love and gratitude, our lives simply transform.

With love

x

193

*A*ccepting life is seen by many as a sign of giving up your power, not taking responsibility. The truth is that acceptance is one of the things that enables us to really take ownership of our life and live the life of our dreams.

Accepting life as it is is not about passively letting go of our life; it is about accepting that our life is as it is and that we have available to us everything we need to shape our life into the life of our dreams.

But if we don't accept life, if we don't accept the abundance of the universe, then we are denying the truth of our world, and any time we are denying a truth, we are accepting a lie. As soon as we accept a lie, we put ourselves out of alignment, into a place of non-acceptance.

And so we come full circle. The non-acceptance is a result of a lie that arose from our denying the truth of acceptance.

Accepting, being grateful and being love are all present in connected souls.

There are no lies in acceptance, gratitude and love. They are all based on truth.

With love

x

194

Many of us live much of our life striving for goals, for rewards, for toys, for representations of wealth, for things or achievements. And there is nothing inherently bad with any of that.

However, there is a misconception that we need to achieve before we can feel good, and this is a lie that is commonly believed. Yet it is this lie that every day leads to millions of people believing that they are not successful, that they are not doing what they should be doing, that they are failures.

It's not the toys or the achievements or the goals that are bad; it's what we've attached to them. We've attached our well-being and the way in which we value ourselves to these external, often material items.

The truth for us all is that we have all we need within us to be happy, to feel blissful, to feel love. We don't need anything external in order to feel our true joy.

We are born with all we need to feel love. We are born joyous and abundant.

Remember, we have all we need available to us every moment of every day.

With love

x

195

*T*aking your life in your hands has typically been associated with someone taking a great risk with their life. The strange thing is that the opposite is true. It is those who don't take their life into their own hands who are taking the greatest risk with their life.

Taking ownership of our way of being, our thoughts, our feelings and our actions enables us to truly accept that we own our life.

The fundamental on which our daily life is oriented is the degree with which we connect with and listen to our heart. When we open up and remember to listen to our heart, our way of being comes from a loving place. Our way of being will then tend to be loving, grateful, abundant, compassionate or something similar.

When our way of being comes from a loving place, then our thoughts and actions come from a loving place. Imagine how the world feels as more people connect with their heart and live with a way of being that originates in a loving place — how the world is transformed!

Own your life from a loving place and be part of the loving transformation that is happening in the world already.

With love

x

196

*T*here appears to be an acceptance and even a promotion of motivation through fear and scarcity.

Remember that the universe is abundant and we get more of what we put our attention into. When we put our attention into fear and scarcity, our lives will certainly consist of more fear and scarcity!

Start to notice the way in which marketing dwells on fear and scarcity to promote products and services. Notice also the way in which many public information announcements are warnings of what not to do rather than encouraging us towards things/activities that would support and serve us.

Live in love and abundance rather than fear and scarcity. Watch how your life blossoms.

With love

x

*O*ne of the beauties of life is that we never know what's around the corner. This unpredictability is something that some of us relish and others of us fear.

I've heard it said that the only certainty is uncertainty, the only thing constant is change. Living in fear of unpredictability is a sure way to compromise the quality of your life. Choosing to embrace change and love the unpredictability of life transforms our life experience.

As children we eagerly sought out new experiences, new adventures. We had no fear of the unknown. We laughed and skipped as we discovered new adventures. To find something new was a cause of joy and excitement, not something to be fearful of.

Imagine how life would be if we were to continue to explore adult life with the same intent as we did as children, finding our way in the playground that we call planet earth! We'd be laughing and skipping instead of fretting and being immobilized by fear.

Explore the adventure of life through the eyes and heart of a child. Remember that life is here for us to live moment by moment. We never know what's coming round the corner so have a blast right now.

Enjoy the ride!

With love

x

Tim Brister

198

*L*ive your life with the certain knowledge that everything is unfolding perfectly.

There is so much amazing information, so many great speakers, so many words of wisdom. Sometimes it can feel like you are not where you're meant to be because everyone else is living a life aligned with all the wisdom you see, hear and read.

Trust.

Trust that you are exactly where you need to be in the journey your soul is undertaking in your human life. Trust and let go of any expectations or comparisons, let go of the aspects of your human existence that don't serve you.

Love.

Love yourself, for you truly are exactly where you are meant to be. Love all those who contribute their wisdom to raise the vibration of us all.

Gratitude.

Be grateful for the miracles of the universe and the gift of human existence.

Trust. Love. Gratitude. Bedfellows for an amazing life experience.

With love

x

199

*T*ake a breath, a moment. Pause and bring to mind one occasion today when you've felt grateful. It can be any thing, person, experience, event that you felt grateful for.

Notice how you felt at that time and how you feel when you bring that occasion to mind.

Now imagine feeling that way all the time, every moment of every day. How would that feel? Is it even possible?

The good news is that, not only is it possible but, it is how you deserve to feel. What's more, to feel grateful is available to all us, it is simply a choice. We can choose to be grateful at every and any moment.

The cherry on the icing on the cake is that as we choose to feel grateful then more of the miracles and good stuff that we're grateful for appear in our life!

Be grateful.

With love

x

Nurture your soul. Your soul is present in your body, your soul is grateful for your body. Be sure to nurture your soul by listening to your body and nurturing your body.

So often we ignore, numb or drug the wisdom of our body. Our human body is a miracle. It knows best how to nurture itself; what we need to do is to pay attention to our body's wisdom and respond to that wisdom.

Your soul has chosen your body for this human experience. Respect and love your soul. Take notice of what your body is telling you.

With love

x

*T*rusting your instincts is advice we might often give and receive. And most of us would agree that following our instincts is a good thing to do.

How consistently do you follow your instincts? How often do you sense something or hear a voice coming from deep inside of you but you ignore it?

The first thing to acknowledge is that you noticed that sense or that voice. That in itself is a great place to be. Then consistently trust and act upon that intuition.

The key is to trust, to trust your intuition and to trust yourself. We really do know instinctively how to be, what to do. If only we would pay attention to and act upon our intuition.

Pay attention, trust, act.

With love

x

202

*S*o many people are overwhelmed by uncertainty and fear, leading them to feel overwhelmed with life. Take some moments today as you go about your daily life and pause to connect with those around you. Connect and get a sense of their state of being.

Don't get distracted by what they're doing. Are they BEING love, gratitude, fear, certain, uncertain, compassion?

The way we are being is pervasive. It comes through every experience irrespective of what we are doing whereas what we do is transitory, what we do comes and goes.

We can do things to distract us from a way of being that we want to numb/ignore. For example, if we feel fearful, we might have a drink, eat some chocolate, watch TV, drink coffee, eat a muffin, etc.

None of those are bad things to do. BUT, what is it that causes you to do them? If it's to get away from a way of being, then it won't work! You will still be being the way you are being until you are being something else! Eating, drinking, watching TV won't change it.

Acknowledge how you are being and decide if that way of being serves you. The magnificent gift of human life is that the choice is entirely yours, in every moment of every day.

Choose from your heart.

With love

x

203

*G*ift yourself the space and time to keep learning. There is so much available to learn, so much that enables us to develop, to remember, to enable us to contribute more to others.

There is so much available that is free, we can freely try different topics, different skills, different learning styles until we come across the combination that works for each of us. Learn about something you feel passionate about, something that excites you and that you'll want to get out of bed for!

Giving yourself the gift of learning not only keeps your mind active and agile but it lets your spirit know that you are nurturing and caring for yourself. There's also something about how it takes you back to being a child, because the most intense learning period for most of us takes place when we are at school. We somehow recall the positive aspects of that learning experience.

Keep learning. Find something that excites you and learn some more. Learning serves us and those we interact with in many ways.

With love

x

204

*T*he universe delivers, it really does deliver, when you decide to be loving, to be grateful. You set your intention according to that way of being and just let go of the process. I've seen so many people have that experience based on the Law of Attraction.

As humans, that whole process is alien to a human way of being. Firstly, we invest most of our time in doing to be rather than being and then doing. When we're being love, being gratitude and THEN doing, we get completely different outcomes compared with when we do first in order to be loving or grateful.

Then there's the intention-setting step. Some of us do that but what we also do is set intentions of things we want to avoid. The universe doesn't differentiate between positive and negative intentions; it just identifies intentions.

The final step of letting go of the process is something that many of us find almost impossible, because we don't REALLY believe that the universe delivers.

All our challenges with the Law of Attraction are based on our human need for certainty. Many of us believe that certainty can only be achieved through control (never mind that control is an illusion!).

Consider this: the Law of Attraction is operating every moment of every day. The question is, will you let your humanness go and experience the beauty of the Law of Attraction?

Be love, be gratitude and believe. You deserve it.

With love

x

Tim Brister

205

*F*or most people life is lived within the confines of their beliefs about how life is "meant" to be and what they believe they can and can't do. So often that way of living is less of a life to be enjoyed and more of an existence to be endured.

The sad thing is that for most people their beliefs about life and their beliefs about their capabilities are not really their own beliefs; they've accepted them from their family, authority figures, peers, role models. What is more, whilst these beliefs about life are often portrayed as truths, they aren't true (unless you believe them to be true!).

The universe is abundant. Life is an adventure that passes in the blink of an eye. Listen to your heart, follow your dreams and your passion.

Whatever you choose to believe about life and about your capabilities, make your own choices and make choices that support you in your life.

Remember, the universe is abundant and miracles are happening every moment all around us. Have an amazing life.

With love

x

206

*A*t our core, at our very heart we are love, pure love. Anything else is an illusion; it is not true and means that we are living out of alignment with our true self. When we are out of alignment, life does not flow with the freedom we all deserve.

We are being love when we let go of the accumulated interference that we have collected during our life. When we are born, we are love, there is no interference. As we make our way through life the interference seems to freely accumulate.

Happily we can choose whether we allow the interference to stay and to dumb down our life experience. It is a choice. We all make that choice in every moment of every day.

I'm choosing love, not interference. What will you choose?

With love

x

207

*I*f you want to know the secrets of sustained success in life, then here are the two most commonly found:

1. Spend less than you earn.

2. Keep providing more value to those you come into contact with.

It really is as simple as that.

You don't need any specific education or to live in any particular location or have any particular background.

We all understand what it means to spend less than we earn. But what does it mean to keep providing more value? That sounds like it could be a bit trickier? Not really...

Adding value is about providing something (written, spoken, felt, etc.) that the recipient feels is of value to them. We all have skills, talents, knowledge, experience, ideas to offer. We all know people who could find those valuable!

Keep providing value and notice what happens in your life.

With love

x

*I*t is so easy and so common that humans overlook daily miracles of life just because they happen every day. With that overlooking of the commonplace we miss so many simple ways to be grateful for our lives and the universe we inhabit.

Just because the birds sing everyday, is that birdsong any less of a miracle of nature? — a miracle of nature that could be a trigger for us to connect with nature and be grateful for all the miracles of nature.

The beating of our heart: something that is essential to our survival as humans, yet it happens without thought everyday of our lives. A miracle we could be grateful for.

The air that we breathe: the miracle of nature's continued production of air for us to breathe.

These are all miracles that we could be grateful for... were we to pay attention to them. The beauty is that being grateful for daily miracles such as these means that we make ourselves more disposed to be grateful for everything that comes into our life.

When we are habitually grateful, there's a magical effect that brings more into our life for which we can be grateful. It's truly beautiful.

Be grateful for what appears commonplace and notice gratitude engulfing your life.

With love

x

Tim Brister

209

*O*ften we'll hear people talk about making a judgement as they form a view on whether they are going to follow a particular course of action, or making a judgement as to whether to take a risk or not.

It's also common that judgement is the word used to describe what we are doing when we are considering how people (including ourselves) are performing. In this context we are invariably judging. Judging usually involves an assessment of whether that person is good or not, whether that person has performed well or not.

When we are judging, we tend to be extremely harsh on the person being judged, especially when we're judging ourselves. Judging tends to be a very destructive process for both the person being judged and the person judging. Because of the harshness of the process it serves neither party. In fact it's toxic.

Notice when you are judging yourself and others, but start with yourself. How does that judging support you? Are you being kind to yourself? Would you judge others with the same harshness as you judge yourself?

Start to notice how judging yourself feels. You might find that you decide to be a little kinder to yourself.

Be kind to you.

With love

x

210

*T*here are occasions when life challenges us. There are occasions when our interaction with others challenges us.

Every challenge is an opportunity for us to become an even better version of ourselves. Some will say that all challenges are opportunities and that changing the way we label them makes all the difference.

In truth, it all depends how we respond to the label we use. We could label these events as anything we choose; for example we could label them challenges, opportunities, gremlins, starfish, or anything we choose. Choose a label for you that puts you in a resourceful place to respond to the event.

Which resources will serve you best? There are many resources within you, and you will know the best ones for you.

A resource that has served many others in this place is love. Being loving of yourself and others is a great place to start.

Respond to your challenges resourcefully.

With love

x

211

"*S*mile and the whole world smiles with you". So the lyrics of a classic song go.

It sounds so simplistic — how can our smile impact on the whole world? Surely that's impossible?

Not only is it possible but it's true! It's true because we all see the world through our own lens, our own filters.

If we look at the world through our own, smiling filter, then we are going to find a world that appears and feels like it's smiling. Our attention will be drawn to notice the smiles of others.

If we look at the world through a grumpy, despondent filter... guess what? We'll find a world that appears and feels like it's grumpy. Our attention will be drawn to notice the despondency of others!

So the lyrics of that old song really do hold true. Notice how simple it is to create a smiling world. Start by smiling!

With love

x

212

*S*ometimes we forget. Everyone is being and doing the best they can be based on where they are and what they know.

If we kept this truth in mind then we would probably be a little kinder/more accommodating to the actions and behaviours of those around us (by the way, that includes ourselves!).

There are many factors that contribute to what we are being and doing.

Accept that everyone is being the best they can be right now in this moment. Send love to everyone and be grateful for everything.

Acceptance, love and gratitude. Live with these in your heart and as your way of being... Your life will transform!

With love

x

213

*T*here are many beautiful aspects of life we can be grateful for. We just need to be open, ready and willing to gratefully receive whatever experiences come our way.

Enjoying the magical miracles that appear in our lives keeps our life force vibrant. Being grateful for all these magical miracles increases our enjoyment of these miracles whilst at the same time expanding the gratitude in our world, how beautiful is that?

Gratefully notice and receive the magical miracles of your life and notice how your life, moment by moment, transforms.

With love

x

214

*T*here is an unpredictability about human life that, if we choose to embrace it, can enable us to live every moment of every day as a bold adventurer! Alternatively, we can allow the unpredictability of life to overwhelm us, so that rather than adventuring boldly, we tiptoe fearfully.

How we respond to life's unpredictability is a choice, a choice that each of us makes every second of every day. To adventure boldly or to tiptoe fearfully — which will you choose?

With love

x

215

*G*ratitude. The more grateful we are, the more time we decide to be grateful, to be gratitude, the more we have to be grateful for... It really is that simple, not always easy, but always simple.

When life is so simple, how is it that we are able to observe so many people being ungrateful so much of the time?

This simple truth of gratitude is not a secret; it is available to all of us, yet somehow the majority of people act like they don't know the truth of gratitude.

There is one word, a simple three letter word that describes how so many people appear to not know the secret of gratitude.

That word is... ego. Our ego knows that once we live in the truth of gratitude then the days of the ego are numbered. There is no place in gratitude for the ego.

Gratitude is all about love and abundance. Ego is all about fear and scarcity.

Gratitude and ego cannot coexist.

Most of us are ruled by our ego, so for most people the truth of gratitude doesn't get a look in.

Let go of your ego. Enable gratitude to shine through for you.

With love

X

*H*ow do you view yourself? Are you a leader or a follower?

Leadership can feel like some massive thing that is way beyond "mere mortals". Is that really true?

Are all leaders not "mere mortals"? We are all humans, we are all capable of acts beyond that which we currently believe. But many people believe that leadership is something for others...

Just consider, if you are a parent, who do your children look upon as leaders? You will certainly be one of them. Amongst your friends and peers have you ever been the one who has taken the lead, perhaps on choosing where to go on a night out, or where to go on vacation?

The truth is that we are all leaders. It's just a question of how big we choose to lead. But rest assured, every moment of every day you are a leader!

With love

x

217

*L*ife can seem to be such a rush, so full of competing demands, so high speed. It's oh so easy to find ourselves rushing and running from one activity or event or interaction, to the next and then the next, never being truly present in any of these events, either reliving the missed opportunities of the previous event or the promised opportunities of the next event.

We do this, believing that by rushing around we are achieving and that we can get more done if we multitask, by being at an event whilst thinking about another event.

Nonsense, absolute nonsense!

The truth is that by taking the time to be absolutely present in the moment, in the current event we will experience the true richness that life has to offer. The more we rush, the less present we are and the more we feel dissatisfied and disconnected... at all levels.

Give yourself the gift of time, the gift of time to be present in this moment. It might feel slower but it's actually a lot faster and a lot more fulfilling.

With love

x

218

*T*here is a simple recipe for a healthy and happy life. It is so simple, yet it's not always easy. We all know the secret. It's a way of being we are born with. We are being this way as we enter the world. The question is whether we choose to carry on being that way.

The simple recipe: To be love.

We are pure love and we enter the world being that way.

Why would anyone choose not to be this way? That's the work of the ego. But today's message is not about the ego; it's about being love.

Choose to be love

With love

x

*W*hen is the right time to give up on your dreams? When do you decide that, actually, where you are is ok, that it feels comfortable and something you're happy to settle for?

Some people give up before they even start. So if you're following your dreams then your chances of reaching them are a lot better than those who have decided to not even start!

There are others who decide that rather than give up, they'll moderate their dreams, just water them down a bit to something more realistic. Realistic has been the death knell to the dreams of billions of people. Let's get honest with ourselves, being realistic when it comes to our dreams absolutely stinks! You're better off being honest with yourself and declare that you're giving up on your dreams. Being realistic is a living death because somewhere inside you the dreams are living under this veil of realism!

There are those who keep their dreams undiluted, with no realism. So they have the big dream, but then they are halfhearted with their commitment to their dreams. They don't truly believe that they deserve their dreams to come true, so they don't do whatever it takes. These are the people who tend to settle for a life that's not as they imagined in their dreams but they feel comfortable. They give up on their dreams.

Then we have those who never give up, and they are fully committed and they do whatever it takes for as long as it takes. These people, they get to live their dreams, all because they believed it was possible and they did whatever it took for as long as it took. It really is that simple.

You can see, there are multiple ways to give up on your dreams. And there's one simple (not always easy) way to guarantee living your dreams.

You get to choose.

With love

x

220

*L*isten to your inner knowing. We all have an inner knowing that senses when we are in alignment. When you're doing something that isn't flowing for you, notice how you feel; listen to what your inner knowing is telling you.

We often refer to having a gut feel or a sixth sense or something similar. This is our inner knowing. The thing to do is to pause our lives for the few moments it takes to listen to our inner knowing.

So often we notice that something doesn't feel quite right or there's a feeling in our stomach that we usually interpret as thirst or hunger (thereby numbing our "gut feel" in that moment). How often do you pay attention to these feelings of dis-ease?

Those feelings of dis-ease are our intuition telling us to look at what we're doing, at how we're being and to make an adjustment, to get us back in alignment. And remember, the slightest adjustment can make the world of difference to you, your life and the experience of those in your life.

Listen to you.

With love

x

*L*ove is the answer. Begin with loving yourself. You were born loving yourself, loving everything and everyone. Love was all you knew. Return to the beginning and return to the perfection of love.

There is so much unlove in the world. Be aware, this is not the same as hate. We are unloving of ourselves, unloving of others, unloving of where we live, unloving of our work, etc., etc.

We had to work hard to push to one side our natural need to love so that unlove could thrive. But most of us do that hard work so we can confirm and be part of the group we aspire to!

How crazy is that? We aspire to be part of the unlove group. We convince ourselves that unloving is the way to be, when all along we are born with love, the greatest gift of all.

Love or unlove: it's a choice.

With love

x

222

*L*istening to your heart, trusting yourself — we know it's the right thing to do, yet sometimes it can feel difficult and lonely.

Keep checked in with your heart. Keep grounded with your true self. Others might not understand; they might try and tempt you away from the path that your heart knows to be true.

Those other people believe that they are doing the right thing for you, but they are acting based on their model of the world, not yours. You do know what is right for you. Your heart knows.

Sometimes it can be tempting to leave our heart and follow another path. In the short term it might feel better on the other path, but our heart really does know our truth. Our heart knows our true path.

Listen to your heart.

With love

x

*H*ow much playfulness do you see every day? How much playfulness do you have in your life on a regular basis? If you have young children in your life then there is likely to be a lot of playing going on, but what about playfulness?

There is much in life that we can take seriously and much that can feel heavy in our lives. Playfulness is light.

Visualise a playful situation. What do you see? Laughter? Skipping? Fun? Escape? Whatever playfulness is for you is right for you, right here, right now.

Decide today that you will be playful every day. For a few moments, be playful. Watch the playfulness expand and spread like an antidote to the heavy issues that can weigh down our world.

Be playful. Laugh, skip and have fun!

With love

x

224

*E*verything happens right now, in this moment. We can invest so much energy and emotion in what might happen sometime in the future or what has happened in the past, but the only moment we have to live is this one, so let's live it!

There are times to plan for the future and times to reflect on and recall the past. Just be sure to be present when you're doing the planning and recalling.

Many of us have a tendency to dwell in the past, to reminisce about the "good old days" or to beat ourselves up about all the "mistakes" we made. Experience also tells us that our memory of the "good old days" is extremely selective, because we forget all the stuff that was going on that wasn't so good. Equally, without the "mistakes" we would not be who we are today.

A question for you... Could you describe your life as a series of experiences? Rather than as a success or a failure/mistake, start to describe everything as an experience. Notice how that feels for you.

Keep present, in this moment.

We hear about living life to the full. One simple truth is that life is only lived one moment at a time.

Live each and every moment to its fullest; that way you'll live the whole of your life to the full!

With love

x

225

*L*oving what is isn't always easy. Loving what is is sure to feel right. Loving what is brings you to the present moment, because all that is is here in this moment.

When you take the decision to be love then loving what is becomes something you do. It becomes easier, it becomes second nature (or maybe, thinking about it, first nature!).

Being love has many other side effects, every one of them beautiful and fulfilling to the soul.

Be love. Love what is.

With love

x

*O*ur human existence offers many, many opportunities to connect with the wisdom of our soul. To keep us on our toes, our human existence also offers us many, many distractions.

Sometimes the distractions feel more dominant to us, and sometimes the wisdom of our soul feels further away than at other times. The truth is that the wisdom of our soul is with us always. Distractions might come and go but our inner wisdom remains.

Our task as humans is to be present and to connect with our inner wisdom, to act in accordance with our inner wisdom, to enable our inner wisdom to shine through.

Then we are choosing when to pay attention to distractions. We are choosing based on the inner wisdom of our soul.

Distractions are not inherently bad. We simply need to be in a position to choose when we pay attention to them, instead of have distractions choose when we are distracted.

Enjoy a life of wisdom. We all have it, we might as well enjoy it!

With love

x

*T*oday, in this moment if there was one thing, one person, one event, one gift, one feeling, one anything that you could feel gratitude for, what would that be?

It doesn't have to be anything huge. It could the smallest thing; it could be something that you've only noticed in the past few moments since you started reading these words. It could be something that's been with you for years.

You might well have noticed several things come to mind, and you are able to feel gratitude for all of those things.

As humans, we are blessed that in every moment of every day we are able to notice something, perhaps many things, to feel gratitude for. In that moment, we didn't have to achieve anything; we simply needed to direct our attention towards whatever we wanted to feel gratitude for!

Being grateful and feeling gratitude really is as simple as that, maybe not always easy but definitely always simple.

The beautiful thing is that gratitude is contagious, and a little goes a long way. Give yourself the gift of gratitude. It will light up your life and the lives of those you interact with.

With love

x

228

*H*ow are your energy levels as you go through your life? How often do you take a moment to notice where your energy levels are? Do you ever put your attention into where your energy is?

The universe consists of energy, and we are energetic beings. So it's probably worthwhile taking a moment to feel the energy in you right now.

As we go through life and have more time on earth, the prevailing thought is that over time our energy levels deteriorate until our human existence ends. It seems that most people not only accept that thought as being true, they also accept accelerated energy reduction!

Notice today your energy. Notice the energy of those around you. Notice the absence of energy both in you and in others. How does that feel?

As soon as we settle for any part of our life being out of alignment with our true passion, then (and whilst we continue out of alignment) our energy is depleted. That's the way most people live; hence the acceptance of accelerated energy reduction.

As humans we are blessed. Because we are energetic beings, this state of reduced energy is not permanent! As soon as we come back in alignment with our passion, then like a spark that reignites the smouldering embers of a fire, our energy fire reignites.

We all know people whose energy levels have increased as they've gotten older. They've uncovered and re-connected with their passion and their energy fire has reignited.

If every day you move towards your passion then your body and your spirit know that. And magically the flames of your energy fire will glow brightly and strongly.

With love

x

*T*here are many people in the world who are dissatisfied with their lives but are not willing to take any steps to make permanent change. This results in a high demand for distraction, for ways to fill time that do not require the dissatisfied ones to connect with their current life.

As a consequence there is much trivia, clutter, noise available for everyone. Much of this clutter easily seeps into the lives of the majority, things like email, TV, web surfing, gaming, etc.

Take a check today on the amount of clutter in your life. How do you feel about the volume of clutter and its value for you? Do you choose how much, how often, when, if you engage in any clutter-related activity?

Keep an eye on the clutter levels in your life.

We all deserve to take care of ourselves and to have balance in our life. Choose your balance, for you and your spirit.

With love

x

*T*here is much written and spoken about our thoughts, our minds, being mindful, and how through our thoughts we can transform the circumstances of our life.

It is true: our minds are remarkable tools with still-to-be-explored capabilities. Yet for all the capabilities of the mind, on its own it is incapable of leading us to our true destiny.

Our true destiny is known to our heart. Once we truly connect with our heart, then, and only then, can our life be in alignment with our true purpose, and only then can love truly flow through us.

That's worth repeating... Only when we truly connect with our hearts can love truly flow through us.

Let your heart be your guide; be love, be gratitude, be compassion. Your mind and your heart are intended to work together in perfect harmony, the mind's wondrous capability providing the perfect tools to follow the heart's lead.

That is the key. Only when our heart is leading are we able to be in alignment with our destiny.

Trust your heart.

With love

x

Tim Brister

*T*he fear of the abundant opportunities available moment by moment is a major contributor to why most people retreat into their own world, a world of disconnection, of settling — a world without passion and love.

What is it we're fearful of? How did we learn to become fearful of the abundance into which we are all born?

Just ask someone who lives without this fear; ask them if they feel excited, passionate about life, and whether they feel wealthy. This is not financial wealth; this is about true wealth, the wealth of unlimited possibilities and joy.

The answer will bounce right back as a wholehearted Yes! Yet the majority of people don't live that way. They live in fear.

Just consider for a moment...

There are abundant opportunities for everyone.

Most people fear the joy of recognising the abundant opportunities that exist.

As a result, most people are existing without love, without joy, without connection.

How can the existence of abundant opportunities lead to such a miserable existence? This is the kind of messed up thinking that is commonplace across the world.

Embrace abundant opportunities. Embrace life. Embrace love.

With love

x

*A*s children we all loved stories — stories from books, stories in movies, stories we created ourselves. There were many stories in our life.

Do we ever lose that attachment to stories? As we reach adulthood and some of us have our own children, we introduce stories to them, just as stories were introduced to us when we were children.

Is it possible that for most people, their whole life is based on a story?

What is true in our life? What is true in our life is whatever we believe to be true.

Is it possible that we could create a story for our life and then repeat that story to ourselves so often that we believe that story to be true? We forget that it's a story we made up, because it's been repeated so many times that we now not only believe it, we know it to be true.

That's how many people lead their life. The question now is, what kind of story did they make up? Was it a story of love, passion, adventure and joy? Or perhaps a tragedy of struggle, pain, anger and misery? Or something else?

What's your story? Are there any aspects of your story (life) that you would adjust?

Because our stories are self created, we can change them at any time! If you'd prefer a love story to a tragedy or an

adventure to a farce, then you can change your story (life) in a heartbeat. How awesome is that?

Choose the story of your life!

With love

x

233

*L*ive your life to the full, with joy, with curiosity, with adventure, with gratitude, with love. Life can only be truly lived to the full with love.

Being love is the key to enjoying a life that flows, one that feels full of joy, that overflows with gratitude. There are human situations that can challenge our way of being. The most loving response to everything is to be love. Irrespective of the situation, ask yourself how you can be more loving. This is the response that not only serves you, but it serves everyone else.

But what does it mean to be love? How do you be love?

Being love is a feeling; it's a way of being from which we do. Being love is not a series of actions. There's no checklist. Being love is much less prescriptive than that. There are many ways to be love, and being love will mean something different to each and every one of us.

You'll know when you're being love because you'll feel it. You'll feel connected, compassionate, open, grateful. What you'll notice is the way in which your life transforms as your relationships transform, your well-being transforms and your passion for life thrives.

Being love is a gift, a gift for you and everyone whom you are blessed to connect with.

With love

x

*L*ive life to the full, treating every day as a precious gift. Live in this moment, and take time to plan for the future, always living in the moment.

All around you, every day, miracles are happening. Design a life for you that involves miracles. Plan for a future that is beyond your wildest dreams. Most of all, design a life based around love, gratitude and compassion.

Live the life of your dreams, simply because you deserve to!

With love

x

235

*T*rust the wisdom of your heart and soul. It is easy to confuse the knowledge in our head with the wisdom in our heart.

Our head tends to be very vocal with its knowledge, which is presented in such a way that it's easy to confuse it with the wisdom that we all have in our heart.

The guidance that we seek is always based on the wisdom of our heart, yet so often the knowledge in our head convinces us to listen to our head and not our heart.

Our head operates out of fear. Fear that it will lose the control that it perceives it has over us. Therefore it will work with its ally, our ego, to keep us out of our heart and in our head.

Our head knows that true wisdom lies in our heart and soul. For our soul is eternal and over time gathers wisdom that overwhelms the knowledge accumulated in the head during this short lifetime.

When you seek wisdom, be sure that it is wisdom that you connect with. If you can hear or feel your head then it might look like wisdom but it is really knowledge masquerading as wisdom. Go a little deeper into your heart and soul, the source of all wisdom.

Connect with the eternal wisdom of your heart and soul.

With love

x

236

*L*ove yourself enough to follow your heart. Trust yourself enough to live with freedom.

Being grateful for all that is, being loving and living with freedom not only lights up your life but it lights up the lives of those you interact with. What a beautiful gift!

The key is to love yourself. Only when you truly love yourself will you be able to trust yourself enough to live with freedom, because you will be certain that you deserve to live with freedom.

Listen to your heart, be kind to you and set yourself free! It's your destiny.

With love

x

237

*T*he divine perfection of the universe never ceases to amaze, every moment of every day. So often we might feel like things are not happening in a way that serves us, but everything is always unfolding in divine order.

Why then, does the universe present challenges? The simple answer is that the challenges we are presented with are gifts from the universe. The more grateful we are for all of the gifts of the universe, the more these challenges become adventures.

How about if challenges became adventures? Simply by being grateful we feel like life is more of an adventure than a challenge. How would that be?

Be grateful. Enjoy more adventures.

With love

x

*A*s humans we are blessed to have the freedom to choose. This gift can at times feel overwhelming as we have so many choices available to us.

We have choices about where we live, how we work, what we wear, who we love, what we eat, when we sleep, what we do. The list of choices seems endless. Then within each of those choices we have many, many options. No wonder that sometimes we can choose to feel overwhelmed with the gift of choice.

Imagine that you had just one choice in any given moment. What would that one choice be?

There is a choice that can provide context for all the other choices. That choice is to choose your way of being, to decide how you will be in that moment.

Deciding to be love, to be compassion, to be angry, to be fearful, to be grateful... Imagine the way in which these different ways of being will impact on all your other choices.

We have the power to choose our way of being in every moment. Choose your way of being. Set the context for your life.

With love

x

*L*ive your passion. Whatever it is that lights you up, live it. You know how it feels to be passionate, to have life and energy coursing through you.

You also know, perhaps all too well, how it feels when you're not living your passion. Which feels better?

The question is, do you believe that you're worthy of living your passion? Do you love yourself, really love yourself enough to let go and live your passion?

When you're living your passion, everything and I mean everything just flows, it falls into place. You have energy levels that you only ever dreamt of, a depth of love and gratitude that brings you to tears, laughter becomes a spontaneous event. You are, quite literally, at one with the world.

If you're not aware of your passion, then begin to notice how you are being in different environments, doing different things, being with different people. Notice when you feel most alive; that's when you're getting closer to your passion. Then set your life up so that you experience those things, people, environments. Notice how you feel, and adjust them and keep adjusting them so that you are continually moving towards your passion.

The truth is that your passion evolves so you can expect your experiences to evolve too.

Step towards your passion each and every day. It's what you were born for.

With love

x

240

*E*ach moment passes in the blink of an eye, to be followed by the next moment. Then, in a blink of an eye, that moment passes too.

We have a choice as to how we perceive each and every moment. We can feel the quickness of the passing of each moment and treat each moment as if it were a scarce resource because of the fleeting nature of it. Alternatively, we can enjoy every moment safe in the awareness that the universe presents an abundance of moments.

That one simple choice will have implications throughout our life! The choice as to whether we feel that the present moment — which is the only moment we ever have — is a scarce or an abundant moment is like night and day.

How does it feel to live in scarcity versus living in abundance? How do you feel that might impact your life? Which makes your heart sing: abundance or scarcity?

Choose. Each moment choose abundance or choose scarcity. Choose wisely, your life experience depends on it!

With love

x

241

*E*very day we all deserve the gift of some moments of peace and tranquillity, some calm amongst the demands of the 21st century.

The pace of 21st century life, fuelled by the incredible technological advances that appear every day, is unrelenting. We would all be well served by some moments of tranquillity.

As humans, we are blessed with the capability to create tranquillity whenever we want to. It can be simply done in any environment through the closing of the eyes and a few long, deep breaths.

Putting your attention on your breath enables you to bring tranquillity to you, for you. Take just a few moments of your day to be tranquil and notice the difference.

With love

x

242

*T*he human body is a remarkable creation. It is so aware of its needs and has many ways to tell you when it needs attention.

The question for you is if or when you choose to listen to the messages of your body.

The extent to which you listen to your body is primarily driven by the extent to which you love yourself. For those who love and accept themselves as they are, the messages from the body are usually heard, received and acted upon.

Be aware that often it's the small messages that get overlooked. For example, we might believe that we feel hungry when our body is crying out to be hydrated, and it simply needs water. We might notice signs of tiredness, yet we turn to caffeine rather than giving our bodies the gift of rest.

Be loving to yourself. Listen to the wisdom of your body. Your body knows what you need.

With love

x

243

*T*oday, for a few moments give yourself the gift of truly connecting with someone else. When someone is talking with you, listen to them. Don't let your mind drift; don't think about how you will respond. Just listen.

The act of listening, of truly connecting with another person, is a gift — a gift for them because it is so rare for anyone to feel truly heard, and a gift for you because when you connect with another you are also enjoying the gift of connecting with yourself.

Sometimes we consider giving a gift but we're not sure if the gift will be well received. The gift of listening and connecting will always be well received, if not by the other person, then always by you.

It can take just a few moments to be present and connect with another. Yet the positive ripples that follow are endless.

With love

x

244

*R*emember that each moment is the only moment we ever have, and keep an ear out for the voice of your ego. Your ego will only ever want to drag you away from the present moment into the temptation of the future or the judgements of the past.

A full, vibrant, authentic life can only be lived in the present, in the only moment we have. When we are being authentic and true to our heart, to our true purpose, then we are living in our heart. In that moment, the ego has no voice; in that moment our heart and soul are the source of our internal dialogue.

When our internal dialogue is coming from our heart and soul, it's loving, it's kind, it's coming from a place of love and compassion. Then our internal dialogue serves us, it serves our higher purpose.

When our inner dialogue comes from our head, from our ego, it's based on fear and scarcity. Neither fear nor scarcity serve our higher purpose; our contribution to the world is diminished and worst of all, a piece of us is lost.

Choose to be in the present moment. Refuse the ego's desire to lure you into the temptation of the future or the judgements of the past.

With love

x

245

*B*e grateful for every moment, for whatever events are taking place in this moment, subsequent moments hold new events.

You might judge the events in your life as good, bad, amazing, disastrous, etc., or you might accept every event as an experience.

However you choose to treat each event, be grateful for every event and you will find that life becomes more about a series of experiences that you accept rather than a series of events that you judge.

When you're being grateful for your life, for every experience in your life, then you'll notice an abundance of love in your life. It's one of the consequences of being truly grateful for every moment: when you're being grateful then love simply flows. It's truly beautiful.

Drop judgement, be grateful, and you will enjoy abundant love.

With love

x

246

*T*here are so many well-meaning, kind-hearted, caring people who are busy doing lots of kind things. Yet there remains a sense of dissatisfaction, a sense that something is not right.

No matter how many good things we do, our sense of well-being comes from our being-well. In other words, it's how we choose to be that provides the context for everything we do.

Because much of the focus of the 21st century is around doing, about what we've done, or achieved, or experienced, the joy of life can be lost, because whilst we are busy doing we are being stressed about all the doing we are going to do.

We might well get lots of doing done but because we are BEING stressed we feel dissatisfied at the end of our doing because every doing experience has been experienced from a place of stress.

To be clear, there is nothing wrong with doing. We are humans and we need to do things. However, the quality of every doing experience is determined not by what we're doing or the outcome of what we've done.

The quality of every doing experience is determined by who we decide to be, and that's a free choice that we have before any doing experience starts.

Choose to be whoever and whatever you want to be, and then enjoy whatever you decide to do!

With love

x

247

*L*ive the life of your dreams. Design your own life. Express yourself. However we want to put it, we are all encouraged to live the life of our dreams, to express ourselves, to live our destiny.

Some of you might look at your current circumstances and say that you can't wait to be living your dream or that once you've moved house or got a new job or left your partner or, or, or... The truth is this: however you feel about your current circumstances, this is your current reality and you can change it in a heartbeat.

Here's a truth you might find hard to take:

Your current reality is completely consistent with your current dream. You are living your dream. It's just that you stopped dreaming big and believing in that big dream.

We are all living our dream. We are living the dream that we believe to be the dream we deserve right now in this moment, even if our current reality feels more like a nightmare.

There is a simple step to take to change our current reality. Design your future, believe in it and start to live it.

Remember the dreams of your youth. How does your current reality stack up against those dreams? Very often, the dreams of our youth consisted of excitement, adventure, happiness and joy. How does your life measure up against those?

Live your life with passion and joy. Unleash the power of your dreams and set the example to those around you. Show them what's possible.

With love

x

248

*O*ne of the many great gifts of being human is that our experience of our circumstances can change in a heartbeat. What's more, our actions, our way of being can act as a catalyst for others to change their experience of their circumstances.

We never truly know how our actions, our way of being impact others. Like a pebble dropped in a pond, the ripples of impact continue way beyond those people that we are conscious of.

From time to time we become aware of the impacts arising from our actions and way of being. Be grateful for these moments of feedback.

Continue to drop your pebbles in the pond. Watch the ripples disappear into the pond, safe in the knowledge that your actions and your way of being are gratefully received and shared many times over.

With love

x

2 1st Century life can feel like it's moving at ever increasing speed with ever increasing intensity. This can lead to a sense of the need to progress rapidly to reach enormously stretching outcomes and goals.

These feelings can in turn lead to a sense of being overwhelmed by the sheer size of the task to reach the goals or perhaps a feeling of inadequacy because you're not progressing quickly enough towards the goals and outcomes.

Notice that what's been described is your feelings. In every moment you have the power to choose the feelings you have in response to any stimulus. In fact you can choose your feelings irrespective of the stimulus!

Therefore, it's not the pace of the 21st century, or the enormity of the goals, or the rate at which we progress. None of those determine our life experience and our feelings.

We determine our life experience because we always choose our reaction and the associated feelings.

You are stimuli independent. Own your feelings.

With love

x

250

*P*ay attention to the messages of your body, of your mind and of your soul. As humans we are blessed to be nurturing and to be nurtured by our mind, our body and our soul.

We are constantly receiving messages from all three aspects of our being. Sometimes the messages we receive feel uncomfortable or unwelcome.

Firstly, receive all messages with gratitude, for the message of your being is the perfect message for you to receive in that moment. Allow the message to be with you and to serve you.

You will have noticed that some messages you receive are to some degree similar to messages you previously received. That's because you did not gratefully receive the previous message and then allow that message to be with you and to serve you.

Be grateful for and accepting of all the messages of your being. Trust that all messages are the perfect message at the perfect time.

We truly are miraculous beings!

With love

x

251

Be loving to you. Give yourself the gift of time, remove all expectations of by when you expect anything to happen.

Remember that time is a completely man made construct, and as such it's meaningless.

Once you've understood and you believe that time is meaningless, then you let go of any attachment to a particular outcome taking place at a specified time. The timing is irrelevant; we cannot control it and we've made it up anyway!

Set yourself free from the illusion that is time. And enjoy your transformation.

With love

x

252

*D*uring our lives we'll likely be impacted by the death of a loved one, or someone we care about will be diagnosed with a disease or illness that compromises their life. Often those events are treated as a "wake up call" to put life into perspective.

That waking up and feeling of a new perspective tends to be short lived. Within minutes/hours/days, our lives return to "normal" and we return to enabling the most minor of events to be blown out of all proportion and almost always in a way that does not serve us!

Why do we do that? Why do we blow things out of proportion at all, but especially in a way that doesn't serve us! It's always our choice about how we respond to any stimulus... Choose from a place of being love.

Why do we also wait for a "wake up call" before recognising what's really important in life when we know that what's important is to love and be love? It's always our choice about how we choose to be in any moment. Choose to be love.

Choose to be love, always, because it really is a free choice that every one of us has in every moment.

With love

x

253

When we let go of details and trust in our heart and soul, then there can be only one outcome. The outcome is passion, joy, love, peace and happiness.

Many of us will have often heard the expression "the devil's in the detail". The typical intended meaning is that we will need to be getting into many, many details before we can be sure about the topic at hand.

How about we take a different view of the same expression? We accept that the devil is in the detail (the nature of "devil" is a subject all on its own). And because we all accept that the devil is in the detail we stay OUT of the detail and trust that our heart and soul know everything that we need.

Trust your heart and soul, let go of details and enjoy the beautiful outcomes that follow.

With love

x

・・・・・・・・・・・・・・・・・・・・・・・・・・・・・・・

254

*F*rantic and frenetic activity is commonplace in the 21st century world we inhabit. The emphasis on more, better, bigger, faster feels like it increases every day.

To what end?

Some believe that we are making and demonstrating progress; others might say that we are being more efficient, that we are able to do more; others might simply point to history and say that it has always been this way. What is your experience?

The common thread to all of this is doing. We are able to do more, to achieve bigger goals, to go faster. None of it relates to being.

Yet it is how we choose to be that sets the tone and context for our life experience.

We can always do more, faster, bigger. But, whatever we do, if we are being ungrateful (perhaps because whatever we're doing is not as big or fast as we want) then our experience is going to feel ungrateful.

Who relishes feeling ungrateful? Is there any joy in being ungrateful? How much love do you feel when you're being ungrateful?

Choose how you'll be and THEN do more, faster and bigger. Notice how your experience transforms.
・・・・・・・・・・・・・・・・・・・・・・・・・・・・・・・

If you're not sure where to start being: Be love.

With love

x

*W*e are so conditioned to live within the confines of time that it's easy to overlook that time is an invention of man.

There appears to be a past, a present and a future. Where do you live? Where is the only place we are alive? In the present moment — now.

We are shown how to attach timelines to events, goals, ambitions. And there is a certain pressure to achieve that can come with setting a timeline. But if we want to be in the flow of creativity, where magic really happens, then setting a time frame takes us away from that creative space.

On a practical level, notice how often you check what the time is. Then ask yourself what you plan to do or be different now that you know the time. More than 50% of the time the answer will be that you'll not change anything as a result of knowing the time. It's simply habit!

Release yourself from the man-made, habitual constraints of time. It's all made up. Set yourself free!

With love

x

256

*F*rom time to time there might appear to be an overwhelming volume of challenges in your life. The challenges might become bigger, more impactful; they might appear to be more personal, more persistent.

The size, volume and depth of the challenges in your life is simply a reflection of how far you've come through your life and recognition by the universe that you're beyond a couple of minor challenges. That you're ready for a collection of sizeable challenges that will enable you to develop and grow to the next level.

The real challenge in all of these challenges is for us to be grateful for our growth to date and that we are being challenged in such a magnificent way to enable us to grow further. The universe knows that there's no success or fail in the challenges themselves; it's the way we are as we receive and meet the challenges that holds the gift for us.

Receive challenges with gratitude. They are always here to serve you. They always arrive at the perfect time and place in your life's journey.

Celebrate challenges with love and gratitude, for they are truly a gift.

With love

x

257

*W*hat's a successful day feel like to you? How about a successful week, or month or year for that matter?

The real question here is, how do you determine whether you've had a successful day? What does success mean to you?

For most people, their emotional (and physical) well-being is strongly related to the way in which these questions are answered. Therefore these questions are central to the lives of many.

In truth, the answer to these questions is going to be different for everyone. It's also true that each of us can decide how we frame the question and the answer. In that framing of the question and answer we can set up our lives for success or for misery or something in between.

If you were to determine that success for you was simply being alive, or perhaps saying a kind word to someone, then how often would your day be successful? Pretty well every day!

If you were to determine success as achieving everything on your "to do" list and exercising and getting eight hours sleep and walking the dog twice, etc., etc., how often would you be able to class your day as successful? Probably not very often.

Set your life up to be an experience that you enjoy. Ask and frame questions that serve you.

With love

x

258

*B*eing anything other than love is being something by which we comprise our true selves. We are born being love. Love is our true being; anything else is a lie to ourselves; we all know that we are born to be love.

Many times love is overtaken by fear. Fear and love are opposites. When we truly love, when we are living as love, there is no room for fear.

Fear is an illusion we manufacture. We create fear. It takes effort to be fearful. Love is effortless; when we are being love it flows naturally and abundantly.

Be true to yourself. Be love, be loving.

With love

x

*W*e are born to live, to truly be alive. We're not born to get by, to struggle through, to be ok. We're born to bring joy to ourselves and to others. The world thrives on an abundance of joy and happiness.

However, the absence of vibrant, loving life is all around.

Every moment of every day we get to choose how our life is. In every moment we can be joyful, we can be vengeful, we can be loving, we can be angry, we can be alive, we can be grateful, we can be anything we choose.

So often we hear people say, "I had no choice," "What else could I do?", "It's the only option I had." Every time we say that to ourselves we reinforce our belief that we don't have the ability to choose.

Yet we ALWAYS have the ability to choose our way of being. That is a free choice that we have for every moment that we are living.

Step into your life of joy. Own your freedom of choice. Choose your way of being.

With love

x

260

Many of us have experienced "heartbreak" in our life. Often this leads to us taking steps to protect ourselves by being less willing to open our heart.

This is tragic and ironic at the same time.

The tragedy is that by being less willing to open our heart we are indeed insulating ourselves from truly loving and passionate relationships, starting with the relationship we have with ourselves. This is one of the reasons why people don't love themselves: because they've insulated themselves from their own love by closing their heart!

The irony is that by closing our heart, we are eliminating the possibility of a truly loving relationship with another. This further compromises our life by eliminating the joy that a truly loving relationship brings to those involved.

Trust. Trust yourself and your heart, live with an open heart. Start by being open-hearted with yourself. Be loving of yourself and others.

With love

x

261

*F*or many people there exists an inner tension between the feelings of the heart and the thoughts of the mind. Indeed, sometimes the tension is so intense that it literally pulls you apart.

Typically your heart and mind do come from different perspectives, both of which are essential for human existence. Your heart has feelings based on love, whereas your mind has thoughts based on logic.

Handling the tension can lead to extreme pain, to breakdown, to addictive behaviour. There can be challenges in this tension.

How about combining the love in your heart with the thinking power of your mind? How about eliminating the tension?

The way to eliminate the tension is to be love, so that love floods through your whole being, through your whole human body. Your mind is no longer separate from your heart because the love of your heart is everywhere.

Your mind now operates within the love of the heart. All your thoughts become bathed in and based on love. Where there was tension, there is harmony.

Bathe yourself in your own love. Live in harmony with yourself.

With love

x

Tim Brister

262

*D*ecisions. We make decisions in every moment of every day. Some decisions we perceive to be "big/life-changing" decisions, others less so.

Which decisions are going to have the bigger impact on our life? To decide where to live, to decide if we start our own business, to decide which route to take to work, to decide whether to commit to a relationship with our partner, to decide how we feel about being called fat, etc., etc.

The truth is that we cannot ever possibly know the consequences of any one decision. Yet still we hear people saying that they have a big decision to make, without any way of really knowing!

Treat every decision with the same respect and importance. Decide from a place of love and connection. First and foremost, notice what feels right in your heart and follow that path. Wherever that path leads will be the perfect way, because it is the way of your heart.

When faced with a decision, open your heart and decide. Really, just decide and trust in the wisdom of your heart.

With love

x

263

We typically schedule our lives on the expectation that our health will not get in the way. In fact we often take our health for granted... until it's gone.

Once we find that our health is not as we would like, then we tend to pay attention to our health with the aim to get back to good health.

The time to pay attention to our health is when we feel healthy, not to wait until we feel unhealthy!

Love yourself enough to take care of your body before your body's cries for help lead to you enduring debilitating pain/ sickness.

The body has fantastic powers of recovery. It's never too late to adopt ways that serve your body's well-being. Start today; nurture yourself with nutritious food and some form of exercise. Your body will thank you in many many ways.

Love yourself, love your body, nurture your health.

With love

x

264

*T*his moment is the moment, the only moment. Why would you not want to be and feel love in this moment?

Of course, when the question is put that way, there is no reason why you would not want to be and feel love. Remember that being and feeling love does not stop us doing all the things we want to do or going to all the places we want to go. So why not be and feel love in this moment?

The question is one that only each individual can answer.

The bigger question is why humanity has got to a place where it is commonplace that we aren't being and feeling love in every moment. We are born as love, yet somehow we forget that along the way.

Let's return the world to its natural way of being, to being love. One by one, moment by moment, be love. Lead the way.

With love

X

265

*T*oday, for a few moments, lift your attention away from human activity and pause. Pause and redirect your attention towards the miracles that surround us all every day.

For many of us, we believe that miracles are rare, perhaps once in a lifetime events. Yet there are miracles all around us, every moment of every day.

There is the miracle of life itself. Our human existence is miraculous at many levels. The way in which our bodies function is miraculous. The miracles of nature surround us — for example, the air that we breathe, the cycles of the seasons, the flight of the bumble bee, etc., etc.

Notice the miracles in daily life and your life becomes more miraculous.

With love

x

266

*B*eing spontaneous is a sure way to keep your life alive, to keep your relationships vibrant to keep your life force strong.

Many of us lead lives that are dominated by routine, and some of us lead lives where the routine becomes our life. How does it feel when your routine becomes your life? How much vibrant energy and passion does that bring up for you? Does it feed or deplete your life force?

There is nothing wrong with routine so long as we live our life from our heart and we use routine to enable us to live a vibrant, passionate life.

Be spontaneous, surprise yourself, surprise your partner. Watch the energy, love, joy flow with abundance as you live a more spontaneous life!

How do you do that?... Don't *do* spontaneity. *BE* spontaneous.

With love

x

*L*ive your life your way. Follow whatever is in your heart and stay true to you.

For those who are listening to their heart or who are ready to listen to their heart, your way of living will resonate. For others their fear filled life will mean that they will not resonate with their way of living.

When you are following your heart, then you stand out from the crowd, you are outstanding. Your friends and relatives will likely try to bring you back to the crowd to rejoin their group, in their comfort zone. They don't do this to hurt you or to bring you down, but they do it out of fear. They are fearful of leaving their comfort zone. The unknown scares them.

Be bold. Be prepared to be seen as the odd one out, the one who doesn't stick with the crowd, because that's how you get to live your life your way, with joy, passion and love.

Be outstanding, be bold, and live your life your way, from your heart

With love

x

*H*ow well are you nurturing your state of well-being? Not just your physical body, but at a soul level, how well are you nurturing you?

Some of us look to others to nurture us through our relationships, or through illness (with the care and attention that comes through treatment of illness), or through antisocial acts that lead to care and attention via social care systems, or we look to others in different ways.

Here's the problem with looking to others to nurture us: It is not sustainable. We need to nurture ourselves, not look to others to nurture us.

For all the time we give up the responsibility to nurture us, our soul knows that. Our soul interprets that as meaning that we don't care about ourselves.

Take care of you. Nurture your heart and soul. Love you.

With love

x

269

*D*ecisions change the course of your life. But how consciously do you decide? How many of your decisions come from your heart and how many from your head?

There's a decision that we all make, every moment of every day. That decision is the decision as to how we are choosing to be in that moment.

It's a decision that has a huge impact on the quality of our life. Yet how many people make a conscious decision about how to be? Answer for yourself...

For most people this is a decision that is made automatically, and largely it's a decision based on external stimuli.

Therefore, for most people, the decision on the way they decide to be is given up to random external inputs! It's not even a question of whether the heart or the head leads the decision making process.

Taking ownership for the decision on how you're choosing to be in every moment will change the way you look at your life.

If you take ownership of the decision on how you're going to choose to be and hand over responsibility to your heart, then you will notice transformational changes in your life.

Take ownership of your decisions. Let your heart lead the way. Be whatever your heart desires.

With love

x

*S*ometimes we feel strangely uneasy or not right or short tempered for no apparent reason. We feel like something is out of balance or out of alignment.

How do you receive such feelings? What state of being do you choose to be, and then from that state of being, what do you do?

There are many types of response to these feelings. Some responses serve us more than others. Whatever your response is, it is the perfect response for you in that moment.

Are you grateful? Grateful that you are alive and connected with yourself sufficiently to notice that something feels out of alignment? Grateful that by noticing how you feel, you are in a position to choose your response? Grateful for the opportunity to develop yourself through noticing this temporary misalignment?

Are you irritated? Irritated that something is not right and that you simply want to make it right? Irritated such that you let off steam at the next person you meet or you grab a beer or a coffee or perhaps you go to the gym? Irritated that this feeling is going to destroy your whole day, therefore you need to find something external to blame it on?

Or perhaps there is some other way of being that you respond with.

Here's the truth. Every moment is a gift, and there is a gift in every moment. Sometimes the gifts are hidden or well wrapped, but there are always gifts.

Breathe, be grateful, love and enjoy the unwrapping of the gift in this moment.

With love

x

271

*O*pen your heart, be love, and feel gratitude flow with abundance through your life.

The key is to open your heart, for you to be open to your heart, for you to listen to and receive the wisdom of your heart.

Your heart communicates with you from a loving place; it's the only place it knows. The very act of you listening to your heart leads you towards love, towards being love.

Once you are truly listening to your heart, when you are truly open to the wisdom of your heart, when you are being love, then gratitude flows. Once gratitude flows you have more to be grateful for and so abundance becomes part of your daily experience.

Remember, it all begins with you opening and hearing your heart.

With love

x

272

*F*eel the joy of contribution! The joy of contributing and the joy when others contribute towards you or something you're involved with.

We are here participating in this human experience and whilst there is so much that we can be and do individually, the power of collective contribution is a joy to behold.

Yet so often we allow the busyness and fullness of our lives to be an excuse for not contributing to our own dreams, let alone the dreams of those around us. We look at all the things we have to do and convince ourselves that we'll do more for ourselves and for others when we have more time, yet that time never comes.

The truth is that we only have this moment and it's always up to us how we choose to be and what we choose to do in each and every moment. The choice of what we'll be is fundamental.

Choosing to be love and compassion in every moment will lead to doing more acts of contribution, because when you are being love and compassion, you are setting yourself up to notice and act upon opportunities to contribute. These opportunities are abundant; all we need to do is to notice and act upon them.

Contribution is beautiful. Being love and compassion sets you up for even more contribution.

With love

x

Tim Brister

273

*R*ejoice in the abundance of choice. Every moment of our human existence, we are blessed with more choices than we can even imagine.

Most of us are aware of many day-to-day choices, such as what we choose to eat and drink, what clothes we choose to wear, which route we travel to work, as well as some less frequent choices, such as where we live, who we live with, whether we choose to raise a family.

But we make many, many moment-to-moment choices without even being conscious of them.

Notice how you're feeling. How consciously did you choose how you are feeling right now? Do you believe that you have a choice about how you feel in each and every moment?

The truth is that we are conscious of many, many choices that we make. We also make many, many choices without being conscious of them.

Choose consciously. It's your life, created through your choices.

With love

x

*A*ny time you allow your state of being to be affected by someone else's actions or their opinion or their state of being, then you are empowering someone else to influence how you feel about your life in that moment.

Some might say that it's common to have your family and close friends influencing your way of being. The question is "Why is that ok?".

There's another question as to how you know that you're allowing only family and close friends to influence you. Do you ever get influenced, for example, when driving if another driver does something that you perceive as being incorrect?

Really, the truth is that our state of being is our responsibility. As soon as we allow our state of being to be influenced by anyone, we are giving up responsibility for part of our life.

Trust yourself, trust your heart, and determine your own state of being. Your heart really does know exactly how you need to be in every moment.

With love

x

275

*R*emember that it really does take only a second to transform your day (week/month/year/life).

No matter how balanced and connected we feel, occasionally we encounter human experiences that disturb our state of being. It's part of being human and exactly what we need to be experiencing in that moment.

Embrace these disturbances for the gift that they are, the perfect gift for us in that moment. Receive the gift and enjoy the perfection of that gift.

Don't dwell on what you might perceive as the negative aspects of the disturbance. In that moment, take the gift and return to your balanced and connected way of being.

Accept the gift of every moment.

With love

x

*O*ften we see humans react to the behaviour, the actions, the beliefs of others. Many times the reactions are nothing to do with the behaviours, actions or beliefs of the other but are 100% about the way of being of the person who is reacting.

What's more, the reactions are invariably directed at the other person, with the likelihood that they too will react. That reaction is also based on their way of being in that moment.

This cycle of reaction does not serve us as individuals or collectively. Let us lead the change!

We are all capable of being leaders and setting in motion a more productive and love-based series of interactions.

The simplest way to lead that change is to have a state of being that is love. Then whatever we are reacting to, our reaction and response will be coming from a loving place.

Love is always the answer and love always holds the answer.

Be love.

With love

x

*T*he gift of space and time. We all deserve to give ourselves the gift of space and time.

The space between our thoughts is a beautiful, quiet space. Often we hear people saying that they need space to think. But we don't need more thinking; there's more than enough thinking going on. What we need is space between thoughts, that is, space to NOT think.

How about creating space between thoughts to enable us to be, to simply be. With no time constraints, we can just be present in that moment.

That's what the gift of space and time is about. It's about creating space without time constraints, a gift for us to be present in that moment.

With love

x

278

*B*eing really honest with yourself is something that the vast majority of people feel that they do on a consistent basis. Is that true? Specifically, is that true for you?

Sometimes (maybe most of the time) we fob ourselves off with excuses and partial truths. Oftentimes we'll construct a "truth" to fit our circumstances even when those circumstances do not come close to our future vision for our lives.

Be honest, recognise the truth. This is not about beating yourself up because you're not living your future vision. This is about you being honest with you about your life, not seeing it better or worse than it is, but seeing it as it is.

Come from a loving place. Love will always demand that you are honest with yourself because to be anything less than honest is unloving to you.

Be love, be honest. See life as it is, with gratitude and love.

With love

x

279

*W*hat's your outcome for today? Are there things you want to do, people you want to see, places you want to go, feelings you want to experience? For each of us it's different.

For some of us our outcome is simply survival, to make it through the day. For others our outcome might be to serve, For others our outcome might be to pass an exam.

How about if we all had a shared outcome for our day an outcome to be more loving? How would that change the world for the better?

We are love, so to be more loving is something that we can all be, because we are love and we all have an abundance of love within us.

One of the most beautiful things about love is that the more loving you are, the more abundantly love flows through your life.

Remember that all of us have outcomes for our day. Most of our outcomes are set unconsciously.

Consciously setting an outcome to be more loving will bring out more love in your life and the lives of those around you.

With love

x

280

*H*ow often do we hear people say that everything will work out perfectly? And how often does that perfect outcome become true?

When we're in the midst of a challenging situation or we feel that the odds are stacked against us, then perhaps we might choose to feel that everything won't work out perfectly this time.

The truth is that everything is working out perfectly in every moment of every day. Even when we feel like the odds are stacked against us or we feel overwhelmed, our feelings are the perfect feelings for us in that moment!

It really is magical, once we've let go of our pre-conceived ideas of what's right for us and accepted the truth that everything is perfect. Then the magic multiplies and expands throughout our life.

Trust in the perfection of every moment. Let magic multiply throughout your life.

With love

x

281

*T*he creative power of humans is completely abundant. Yet as many of us travel through our human experience, we convince ourselves that there are creative people and that we're not one of those types of people, because we're not artists or designers or writers...

What a load of nonsense! We are all born with abundant creativity. As children we are creative about everything. When we are asked to tidy our room or do our homework or eat something we don't want to eat, as children we have a never ending number of reasons why we won't be doing those things. There's no question of us wondering if we are creative enough to come up with a reason; our creativity simply flows.

All that happens as we experience more of life is that most of us express our creativity less. The creativity still exists, but because we exercise that part of our being less, it loses power, which we interpret as meaning that we are not creative. Not true! We are all always creative.

Exercise your limitless creativity. Rediscover the creativeness that is bursting to express itself.

With love

x

*T*here is an innate knowingness that all humans are born with. It's intuition, gut feel, instinct. There are many names for this sense of knowing that we all have inside.

At some points in our life we will acknowledge the existence of this knowingness. Oftentimes this will be when we look back on something that did not go as we might have hoped. We'll say "I felt something wasn't quite right" or "My instinct was telling me something was wrong" or "I wish I'd have paid attention to my instinct!".

There will be other occasions when we have acted on our instinct/gut feel/intuition and we've looked back with joy that we did so.

Pay attention to your instinct, trust your gut feel, act on your intuition. We really do have an innate knowing and the world would be a far more connected, loving place were more people to trust that innate knowing.

With love

x

283

*T*here is magic and there are miracles all around. To see them we just need to adjust the way in which we decide to show up in any given moment. Then the magic and miracles of that moment will appear as if for the first time, though they were there all along.

The universe is abundant with magic and miracles. Each of us sees our own magic and our own miracles. Furthermore, we can share an experience with others and come away with completely different memories of the experience, depending on how we show up to that experience.

You really are creating your own reality of every life experience and your reality is determined by how you show up. For example, do you think that when you show up being loving and grateful that your experience will be very different to your experience when you show up being frustrated and angry?

Remember to create your own reality by showing up in a way that serves you.

Remember that how you show up will influence the miracles and magic that you notice in your life.

With love

x

With Love

*B*e open. Be open to explore and experience whatever life has to offer.

The more open you are, the more opportunities you'll find appearing in your awareness. The more opportunities you experience, the more open you'll become.

In each moment there are new experiences to be explored, yet many people are placing their awareness on the avoidance of risk, of danger, of harm.

This is not to suggest that we should all be deliberately seeking to harm ourselves or others or to place ourselves in danger. However, the sad truth is that many people's lives end way before their body dies. Lives end when we stop being open, we stop taking risks, we stop exploring different/ new experiences.

Live your life. Be open to experiences, whatever life throws at you, safe in the knowledge that it's living that keeps you alive.

With love

x

"*F*eeling the wisdom of your soul." What does that really mean? How do we do that? How do we know when we are doing it? Is it even a good idea?

Most of the time, most people live in their heads, where there exists an amazing amount of knowledge and experience. Our heads are capable of storing and recalling huge amounts of complex data that is a fantastic asset in our human existence.

Our challenge, as humans, is to utilise the awesome capabilities of the head within the context of the wisdom of our heart and soul.

From a young age we acquire knowledge and we're rewarded for being able to store and recall knowledge on demand. Generally speaking, we are not educated in the value of the wisdom of our heart and soul. Yet the knowledge in our mind is of much more value to the world when it is called from the wisdom of our heart and soul.

How do we do this? We let go of thoughts, we clear our mind. Instead of having a full mind (being mindful) we empty our mind to provide space for the wisdom of our heart and soul to manifest.

This might sound strange. It might feel counter intuitive. Try it and see how it feels for you and notice what outcomes you get.

Truly, we have all the wisdom we ever need within us now. We simply need to clear space for the wisdom to reveal itself.

With love

x

286

*T*he apparently mundane nature of many people's human existence does not serve the soul of any individual or the collective souls of the planet. We all have joy and love in our hearts, joy and love that is bursting to be shared with others.

Many of us restrict the amount of love and joy in our lives because we are fearful that displaying love and joy leaves us vulnerable to being taken advantage of and/or not taken seriously. But the opposite is true.

Take a moment now to breathe and connect with your heart, really feel the love in your heart and allow that love to flow through your body. You are being love for no reason other than you are choosing to be love.

How does that feel? Does it feel vulnerable or weak? Or does it feel centring and grounded? Being love is the most nurturing and centring way of being that we can be. There is no weakness because it is our true way if being. By being love we are being true to ourselves, to our heart and soul. With that depth of connection we are strong, much stronger than any physical strength: this is a heartfelt, spiritual strength.

Be joy and love. Share your truly strong self with the world.

With love

x

*S*ometimes we can feel like there are fewer hours in the day than there are draws on our time. This feeling can develop into a feeling of being overwhelmed, of fear and anger.

At times like these it is often that we have simply forgotten the truth. That truth is that inside of us we have all that we ever need at every moment of our lives. The question is whether we are going to choose to access all our powers in this moment.

So you can see that a feeling of being overwhelmed is a choice, a choice that we make when we choose not to access the full range of powers that we have inside.

You choose, being overwhelmed or not, it's up to you.

With love

x

288

*T*he richness and diversity of life is a joy to be relished. The constant challenges and battles of life are the cause of our pain.

Both those sentences describe two differing experiences of the same life events. The question is, which one is true?

The answer wholly depends on the meaning you attach to these life events. And that is a choice, a choice we all make in every moment of every day.

The meaning you attach to any event is based on a number of factors. Of those factors, when experiencing the event, the way you are being is fundamental. And you choose your way of being in every moment.

It really is up to you whether your life events are a joy to behold or a cause of pain. Choose from your heart and all will be well.

With love

x

*C*reativity — what does it mean to you? Do you believe that you are creative? Is creativity something that you perceive as being important in your life?

We all have our own thoughts and feelings about creativity. We all have our own answers to those questions about creativity.

How do you feel about creativity when you know that you are creating your reality in every moment of every day? Because this is the truth; you are the creator of your life experience.

Creativity and creation are an integral part of our daily lives, yet there are many, many humans who believe that they are not creative. They believe that creativity is something that others have. How do you think that belief might affect the life that these people create for themselves?

We are all powerful creators with creativity flowing through us in every moment. Enjoy your creativity, enjoy the expression of your creativity, and share your creative nature.

Believe you are creative, because you are!

With love

x

*Q*uestions have power. What questions do you habitually ask yourself and how supportive are those questions for you?

Most people would find it hard to believe that they ever ask themselves nonsupportive questions. Firstly, take time to notice the questions you ask yourself, particularly when you feel challenged or you're having an emotional response.

Then be honest with yourself about the extent to which those questions support you.

Notice that when you ask questions from the place of being love, the questions will always be supportive for you and everyone else, because love knows nothing except love.

Imagine what love would do, and ask questions from that place.

For example, a great question to ask is "What is the most loving thing for me that I can do right now?". Another great question is "What would be the most loving action that I could take right now?".

There are many great questions that come from a place of love.

With love

x

*A*ppreciate this moment for what it is. It is perfect, it is divine, it is now. It is the only moment you have.

Appreciate this moment, being truly grateful for everything that this moment holds. Notice how being grateful feels for you. Notice how this moment takes on new levels of grace and love when you are truly grateful for this moment.

We all deserve to truly live in the beauty of each moment, to be 100% present in each moment. We deserve it for ourselves and for the world at large.

Live your life in this moment, with gratitude, love and joy.

With love

x

292

*H*ow often do you acknowledge or thank others for their achievements or their contributions or for simply showing up? There are times when we simply forget or perhaps we are so wrapped up in our own stuff that we forget to recognise the contribution of others.

Yet whilst there are occasions where we overlook the contributions of others, we do at least recognise and acknowledge their contribution.

The question is, how often do you acknowledge or thank yourself for your achievements or contributions or for simply showing up? How often do you give yourself a pat on the back for being you?

Most of us are far more consistent with our acknowledgement and thanks to others than we are with ourselves. Yet by developing a habit of consistently, genuinely and lovingly acknowledging us, we nurture ourselves and our capability to acknowledge others.

Take care of you. Love, thank and acknowledge you.

With love

x

293

Many people believe they know what it will take for them to be happy/satisfied/better. Then they make it such that they will become happy/satisfied/better only once something has happened or something has changed.

We'll often hear, "I'll be so much happier when I've been on holiday" or "It will be better once the housework is done" or "I'll be satisfied once we've got the house we really want" etc., etc.

All too easily we hand over our state of well-being to outside influences, to the completion of tasks, to the attainment of material items. Our state of well-being is our responsibility; it's ours to own and determine.

In every moment of your life you are determining your state of being. It's always your choice as to how you choose to be in each and every moment.

Lead the way. Decide on your state of well being.

With love

X

294

*C*ontribution is a simple way to enhance the vibration of the world, starting with your vibration. We never get to understand the full implications of our acts of contribution, but we can be sure that the implications extend way further than we ever imagine.

There is a reward that comes to those who contribute from a place of gratitude and service. This reward is all the more beautiful because contribution is an act for which reward is neither sought nor expected.

Yet the true rewards of contribution go way beyond the contributor. The way in which the world is connected today means that the knock-on effects of contributions travel the world at lightening speed.

If ever you feel like you have nothing more to give, then that is the time to definitely contribute. The world is ready and waiting for your contribution, right now.

With love

x

295

*O*pen and expand your awareness. There is so much around us that is beautiful and miraculous. Most of the time, most people walk right by the beauty and miracles that surround us every day.

How often do you take a moment to pause, breathe and notice what is around you? There is unlimited beauty and miracles created by nature and created by humans, most of which we take for granted.

Noticing the beauty and miracles that surround you naturally opens up your awareness and appreciation of life. This increased awareness and appreciation inevitably means that you feel more connected and grounded.

Notice and enjoy the miracles and beauty of life. Expand your awareness in every aspect of your life.

With love

x

296

*L*iving from a place of gratitude and abundance is a beautiful place to be. However, it is not challenge free. It just means that your challenges are very different to those encountered in a place of ungratefulness and scarcity.

The challenges of scarcity and ungratefulness are all about fear, pain, lack, blame. These are low level challenges and are a sign that you are not living in gratitude and abundance. Rejoice in these challenges and what they are demonstrating to you. Moving to a place of gratitude and abundance eliminates these types of challenges.

The challenges of gratitude and abundance are typically around growth, choice, collaboration. These types of challenges are also to be rejoiced in as they demonstrate that you are living in gratitude and abundance.

Rejoice in your challenges. They really are presented at the perfect time to serve you.

With love

x

Where do you live? Which is your habitual home, your head or your heart?

We all have times when we are primarily in our heart and times when we are primarily in our head. The question is, where do you call home — head or heart?

We all have one that we tend towards, and for most people it's their head. We live in a world where thinking (head) is highly valued, yet the true magic of our human existence comes from being in our heart.

It is all too easy to lapse into the mindful, head-led, thinking world where true joy, love, connection and gratitude are nowhere to be found. There might appear to be representations of joy, love, connection and gratitude but they are not true. Only when you are in your heart do those truly come alive.

When you live in your heart then the mind is a tool of the heart; it is led and directed by the feelings of the heart, and that is the way it is meant to be.

Really connect with your heart now, and ask yourself whether it is your home. For home truly is where the heart is.

Let the feelings of your heart direct the thinking of your mind.

With love

x

Tim Brister

298

*H*ow often do you hear yourself or someone else say that they're not sure what to do but that they will work it out?

How does it feel to work something out? It might feel rewarding to have figured something out, like solving a puzzle or a problem. But how connected to your heart does that feel?

Our heart works at a different level than our head. Our heart operates much more deeply and is where we remember the responses that best serve us, irrespective of the question.

At our core we are love and the only way of being that our heart knows is love. Therefore, any response that comes from our heart has to be aligned to our true self, which is why the responses of our heart always serve us perfectly.

Rather than work stuff out in your head, release the magic magnificence of your heart.

With love

x

299

*E*verything, absolutely everything happens in our lives in divine order with perfect timing. Sometimes that will be hard to believe, but that's because we're letting the expectations and fear of our ego interfere with our life.

Whenever you feel that your life is not unfolding as you would prefer, remember it's just the fear of your ego doing all it can to disrupt your life.

Your ego knows that everything is happening in divine order with perfect timing, but it believes the way for it to maintain the illusion of control is to keep you living in fear of your true destiny.

Thank your ego for showing up and for looking after you. Then move right along with your life and into your destiny.

With love

x

300

*W*hat we believe has a huge bearing on the outcomes we experience in our lives.

As humans we are extremely adept at finding ways to prove ourselves to be right. This often means interpreting outcomes in such a way that the outcome is consistent with our beliefs.

Whether you believe something is easy or something is difficult, you'll usually be able to demonstrate through your experience that your belief is true.

Therefore what we believe has a huge bearing on our life experience. For example, two people can go through the same experience and have completely different outcomes because of their beliefs about the experience.

When did you decide what your beliefs were? For most people, beliefs about life are acquired in a haphazard way from parents, teachers, friends, the media, role models, etc. Very few people actively choose what they want to believe about life, yet what you believe is fundamental to your life experience.

Your true beliefs about life are found in the truth of your heart. Listen to your heart and reshape your entire life experience.

With love

x

301

*R*emembering to use language that serves you and those around you can make a real difference to the quality and depth of your life. It is often more comfortable for us to communicate with others in a way that resonates with us, even though that might not be most useful for everyone in that moment.

For example, if you are someone who most values thoughts, you are most likely to be interested in and ask about what others might be thinking or what is in their head. If you're asking that question to someone who is much more instinctive, then they might search in their head for the answer, but for them that's a place where the answer doesn't exist because they rely on the instinct of their heart. Whereas if you ask that same person how they feel about the same topic, then they will immediately access their source, i.e. the instinct of their heart.

This is not to suggest that you need to know everybody else's personal way of internal processing but that you can engage with others in a way that enables them to access their source, wherever that may be.

Use opening up questions and watch your life and the life of those around you expand to greater levels of awareness and passion.

With love

x

302

*G*oing with the flow. What does going with the flow mean to you?

Going with the flow is an act of surrendering to the flow of the universe, the universal flow. How does that feel for you? How does it feel to surrender to the flow of the universe?

For many this surrender feels like a weak act of submission, of surrendering their personal power and hoping for the best. It means the letting go of the control they believe they have in their life and leaving everything to chance.

For others, this surrender is welcomed. It is welcomed safe in the knowledge that we truly do not control our lives, that control is an illusion of our ego. Surrendering to and fully participating in the universal flow is magical because the universal flow is where magic happens.

The universal flow is where we exist, and it's going to carry on flowing; we might as well participate fully in the ride!

Surrender to the universal flow, let go of the illusion of control, and enjoy the magic that follows.

With love

x

303

*A*ccept what is. So much of the pain and suffering in the world today is because most people refuse to accept what is.

It is futile to do anything other than accept what is. Because it is!

Yet time and again our ego mind tells us that acceptance is wrong, because the circumstances do not match the ego's map of what it believes to be perfect. Then our ego mind keeps us in resistance to the truth.

The ego believes that acceptance is the first step towards giving up our capability to change our circumstances. Quite the opposite is true.

By holding us in resistance our ego leaves us in a position where we are out of alignment with what is. From a place of non-alignment our capability to act on our circumstances is neutralised.

Therefore, as is often the case, the actions of the ego have the completely opposite outcome to their intent. Instead of being empowered to change our circumstances, our ego's actions have disempowered us!

Far simpler to accept what is, to keep in alignment with the universe and to then act.

With love

X

304

Recognise that there is only ever one moment, the present moment. Anything and everything else is an illusion.

Yet most people direct their attention to anywhere BUT the present moment. Why is that? What is there about the illusion that is more appealing than the reality?

As soon as we direct our attention away from the present moment we give up our power to the illusion. We are no longer conscious of the truth because we have directed our conscious, thinking mind to some other place of illusion. Typically the illusions will come from our memories of the past or our imagination about the future.

Through directing our attention away from the present we believe that we escape from our responsibility for our way of being in that moment. But the truth is still the truth and the truth will always out.

Directing our attention towards the illusion is merely a temporary distraction that means we are powerless to act in that moment. What's more, every moment we live in illusion is a moment that we haven't truly lived; we are literally deciding to not live our life!

Live your life. Inhabit the present and not the illusions of the past or the future.

With love

x

305

*T*reat life as an adventure. Explore and embrace new experiences, particularly those that feel challenging. As your life unfolds, continue to discover different places and activities.

As children, we have dreams, we treat every day as an adventure. We relish change and any opportunity to do something new and different.

As we move through life, we typically lose sight of our dreams and become less open to change and adventure. Yet we know when we feel most alive: it's when we're doing something we love and life is an adventure.

It's so sad that most people don't even know what their passion is, let alone give themselves the opportunity to follow their passion.

Keep exploring, continue embracing new experiences. For it is there that you'll uncover your passion and with it your zest for living.

With love

x

306

*C*ontinue to be yourself. Every day find ways to be more and share more of yourself, your true self. The world is overrun with misaligned, disconnected people who are not being themselves; they are hiding behind their facade.

Every time you hear yourself speak your truth or you feel yourself acting in alignment with your truth, then your light shines more brightly in the world. The more brightly your light shines, the more others are encouraged to shine their light and the more bright lights we have shining in the world.

Every time we silence our truth or we act out of alignment with our truth we dim our light and we strengthen the facade behind which we live.

Our truth is always based on love, so to speak or to act upon our truth is always a loving way of being. The world thrives when more people share the love that they all are.

Be true, and shine brightly from your truth, from love.

With love

x

307

*L*istening to your heart, to the true you always serves you and everybody else. Be sure that you have really accepted situations or circumstances or behaviours.

With acceptance and the truth of your heart, you can be sure that whatever actions you take really will serve the greater good. For everyone.

With love

x

308

*W*e live in a world where there is an abundance of gifts in every moment. Our choice in every moment is where we place our attention and therefore which of the available gifts we notice.

Where we place our attention and what we notice have a huge impact on our life experience. The meaning we attach to each and every life experience is completely ours, because nothing has any meaning except the meaning we give it.

Sometimes the gifts in an experience might be well hidden and badly wrapped. But when we absolutely know that the universe is abundant and that there is an abundance of gifts in every moment, then we will experience each moment as a gift.

One of the most amazing aspects of the universe is that the gifts never run out or become less available. The gifts of the universe are truly abundant; they continue to flow... The question is how many you'll notice and how that will impact your life experience.

Rejoice in the abundant gifts of the universe!

With love

x

309

*A*t our essence we are love. At the heart of our being we want to express our love, first and foremost our love of and for our self and then for everyone. It is through love that our true connection is formed.

The way to form that true, love-based connection is through the opening of our hearts, through stepping into that vulnerable place where we open our hearts.

There are many people who are so fearful of getting "hurt" that they believe in their heads that the best thing to do is to protect themselves by keeping their heart "safe". The really sad thing is that this idea of protecting the heart to keep us safe is a myth. It has the opposite effect!

Every moment that we are "protecting" our heart, we are keeping ourselves from being alive, we are not living. Because it is only through the opening and expression of our heart that our love flows and that is when we are truly living.

The world thrives when more of us express our true selves through love. What's more, we all deserve to express our true selves through love.

Trust your heart. It desires to be open and for your love to freely flow. Your thinking mind might think that protection of the heart is the way, but it isn't. Your heart always knows the truth.

With love

x

Tim Brister

310

*T*he power of contribution is something that we all intuitively know. Yet so often our thinking mind convinces us that we'll contribute when we have a bit more for ourselves first.

Whether that "bit more" is time, money, compassion, food or anything else, the illusion our mind creates is based on scarcity, based on the false belief that the gifts of the universe are in some way limited and therefore we need to be sure that we have our "fair share" before we are able to contribute beyond ourselves.

As is so often the case, the thinking of our minds is the exact opposite of the truth of the universe. The truth is that because the universe is abundant, the more we contribute, then more of whatever we contribute is available to us!

Contribution is one of those human acts that is wholesome and fulfilling for all involved.

Contribute.

With love

x

311

*H*ow often do you acknowledge you? The magnificent beauty that you are, the wondrous talents that you bring to the world, the love that you share, the contributions you make, the people you support — the list is endless.

How often do you give yourself the gift of truly appreciating all of you? There might even be aspects of you that you believe are not perfect (the truth is that we are all perfect even with our imperfections). Acknowledge those aspects too!

Most of all, enable your love to flow through you. Love yourself, love everything about you, and notice that love is abundant. It is everywhere. During every moment, love abounds.

You are complete, you are perfect. Accepting you enables you to accept everything.

With love

x

312

A simple smile. Do you habitually smile or do you tend to scowl, frown, grimace or something else? What does your habitual expression say about you?

A genuine, heartfelt smile is so different to the fake, picture-posing, cheesy grins that many people wear. As with anything that comes from your heart, a heartfelt smile is beautiful and full of love.

When you are connected with your heart, then smiling becomes a completely natural expression, a heartfelt expression that is immediately recognised by others.

When you are truly coming from a heartfelt place, then you feel whole, you feel content, you feel love. Your whole being radiates with an energy that draws others to you. They might express it by saying that you have a lovely smile because that's a physical manifestation of your energy, which is what's really drawing them to you.

Allow yourself to freely smile from your heart, and notice how your daily interactions transform. It's a beautiful thing.

A heartfelt smile is a beautiful thing.

With love

x

*H*ow connected do you feel to the abundant energy of the universe? We are energy, everything is energy, any disconnection from the energy of the universe is a disconnection from some part of ourselves.

How vibrant and alive do you feel? Look around you and notice how vibrant and alive those around you are. The level of vibrancy and life is an indication of how well in tune your energy is with the energy of the universe. The same applies to those around you.

Many, many people depend upon external stimuli to experience what they believe is vibrancy and aliveness. The truth is that true vibrancy and aliveness comes from within, when our energy is in alignment with the energy of the universe.

Allow your energy to flow freely and your life becomes truly vibrant and alive.

With love

x

314

*O*ne of the often-repeated myths of human life is that we need something, whether we believe we need something material, or a particular kind of relationship, or our body to look/feel a certain way, or to work in a certain job, or to not need to work, etc., etc.

The real truth is that we are all born knowing everything we need to know and with everything we need. We have that within us for every moment of our life. We have everything we need within us for that moment.

Yet so much dissatisfaction, so much disease, so much anger, so much frustration comes out of our mistaken belief that we do not have everything we need within us for every moment of our life. All that pain and suffering is based on an untruth!

Of course, we can desire material items, different jobs, different shaped bodies, etc. But we need none of those things, because we have all we need within us now and in every moment.

And we already know that we don't need anything; we know in our heart that we have everything we need within us for this moment. Yet we allow the wisdom of our heart to be overrun by the needs created in our head.

Next time you feel that there is something or someone missing from your life, take a breath and remember that right now you have everything you need within you.

With Love

Listen to your heart. Trust that you have all you need.

With love

x

315

*O*ur unbounded creativity is one of the beautiful elements of our life. We are all miraculous, creative beings. The question is to what extent we empower and express our creativity and for what cause or purpose.

Sadly, many of us learn to believe that we are not creative, that being creative is something for others, not for us. With that belief, we reduce the amount of our creativity we share with the world.

The truth is that we are all abundantly creative and that we deserve to express our creativity and that the world benefits from us all expressing our creativity.

Remember and believe that you are abundantly creative, and express your creativity. Every moment that you deny your creativity you are denying a part of you. Every moment that you deny a part of you is a moment that you've not been fully alive.

Every moment is here for you to live it fully. Express your creativity as you live life to the full.

With love

x

316

*A*s three-part beings we need to keep our attention on nurturing all three aspects: our mind, our soul and our body. From time to time we allow our attention to drift away from our whole being. Fortunately, our being notices and always provides reminders or warnings that are intended to bring our attention to where it is lacking.

The question is how we respond to the reminders we receive. Do we even notice? Do we ignore them for a while until they get more severe?

Many of us resort to distractions, to drugs, TV, alcohol, food. Whatever distraction we choose, all we are doing is masking the symptoms, and the root cause of our discomfort is left to blossom. In effect we are nurturing the very thing that our being is warning us about!

Take care of you, every aspect of you. Listen to your being. When you receive the messages from your being notice and act.

With love

x

What's your story? We all love a good story. What's the story that you habitually repeat that you use to describe why you are where you are and why what is happening is happening?

Where has your story come from? Is it something that you consciously constructed because it serves you in this moment? Or maybe it's a story that has evolved based on the stories of others such as your family, friends, peer group?

Notice your story. What's your role? Are you the hero/ heroine, the warrior, the leader, the child, the victim or victor, the lover, the betrayed, the betrayer? What's the role you habitually repeat and embed in your being?

Very often, the stories that don't serve us are stories that support and reinforce our belief that we would be this were it not for that, and that is something we can't control so it's really not our fault if we are not this.

Any story that places ownership/control of our situation outside of ourselves is a story that disempowers us. It does not serve us.

The thing is that stories are just that: they are stories. We've made them up! The great thing about knowing that stories are made up is that we can always dispense with the old, disempowering stories and make up new, empowering stories that serve us!

After all, if we're going to make stuff up and believe that stuff, we might as make up stuff that serves us!

Create new, empowering stories for your life. And when you fancy a new story, you can make up a new one.

With love

x

318

*H*ow often do you listen to the advice of others? How often do you listen to your thoughts? How often do you listen to the wisdom of your heart?

How often do you act on whatever it is you are listening to, irrespective of the source?

Being aware of the source of the advice/wisdom/judgement you pay attention to enables you to begin to notice how much you value yourself over others and how connected and aligned you are with your heart.

The true power and sustainability of actions comes when our actions are aligned with the wisdom of our heart.

Being aligned with the wisdom of our heart is just that: it's a being, not a doing, and that is the key. Being in our heart enables us to be sure that what we are doing is serving us and serving others, because it's coming from our heart.

Notice the source that you most frequently listen to. Know that listening to the wisdom of your heart is when your actions are best aligned with your core.

With love

x

*H*owever you are feeling, whatever is in your mind, take a moment to notice what in your life you could be grateful for. The wondrous beauty of our world and of our lives holds unlimited causes for us to be grateful. The question is, where will you place your attention?

There are times when we allow our attention to dwell on aspects of our life that we might see as challenges or problems. We are humans and that happens. The question to ask yourself is, what are the gifts in this challenge/problem/situation?

Once we identify the gifts, then we are placing our attention on things for which we are grateful. Being grateful completely transforms our experience of the situation; our attention naturally shifts away from the negative aspects towards the gifts we are experiencing.

Living this way enables you to be increasingly grateful for the gifts in your life.

The universe is beautiful. What you'll notice is that the more true, heartfelt gratitude you feel, the more easily you'll notice the flow of gifts through your life, for which you'll be grateful!

With love

x

320

*B*e kind to you. Ask yourself, how kind are you to you? We so often defer the nurturing of ourselves as we invest so much energy and love in nurturing others.

We all want to serve, to support others, to contribute. The truth is that, in order to serve others we need to first take care of us. If we are not strong and healthy, then we will not be capable of serving others, thereby denying ourselves and others of a beautiful gift.

It is a gift for us to serve and contribute just as much as it is a gift for those to whom we serve and contribute. But the first gift must be to ourselves, the gift of being kind to us.

Remember to sleep well, to eat well, to move well, to feed your mind, to nurture your soul and most of all to love yourself. Be gentle with yourself, speak kindly to yourself, and love you as you are.

Be kind to you, love you.

With love

x

321

*L*isten to you. Listen to your truth. Then act on your truth, whatever that may be and however challenging that might appear to be.

Being true to you means that you are in alignment with your heart, where your truth is to be found. Every time you deny your truth, you add another layer to the layers under which your true self is hidden.

Our truth always exists, it remains with us always. Some of us doubt the existence of our truth because of all the layers of broken promises, missed commitments and lies that we have made with ourselves throughout our life.

Yet because our truth is always with us, we can always return to our truth; we simply need to sweep away the layers of self-deception under which our truth is submerged.

Listen to the truth in your heart. All it needs is to be heard.

With love

x

*H*ow do you view your life? Are you living for the weekend or maybe for your vacations or maybe for the next cup of coffee? Or perhaps every moment is a blessing, every challenge is a gift, every day is abundant with love and life?

The way you expect your life to be is how it will be. If you believe that you are living for the future (be that future a weekend, a vacation, a coffee...) then your attention will be directed towards the future and you will miss the present, your life will literally pass you by. Life only exists in the present; the only moment that we can live is the one we have right now. Give yourself the gift of the present moment and live right now.

Giving yourself the gift of living in the moment builds your belief that every moment is a blessing, that every challenge is a gift, that every day is abundant with love and life. These are all firmly rooted in the present, when life is there to be lived.

Gift yourself the present moment. Live in the abundance of love and life.

With love

x

323

What's important in our life is different for each of us. What's important in your life? How do you decide what's important and what effect does that have on you?

What's important changes as we progress through life. The question is how active are we in determining what's important? Do we allow ourselves to be buffeted along by life? Do we decide what's important to us and then act out of alignment with what we've decided is important? Or perhaps we decide what's important and act in alignment with whatever we decide is important.

If you're living out of alignment with what you believe to be important, then you've allowed what's important to be determined in your head, by your ego. Your ego does not align with your true self; it does not align with your heart.

When you're living in alignment with what's important, then you are in flow. What's important has come from your true self, from your heart.

Trust your heart to know what's important for you, every moment of every day. Your heart lives in the present, which means that you are always in alignment with your truth, as that truth develops through your life.

Listen to your heart.

With love

x

Tim Brister

324

*L*ook around. Look around and see everyone going about their lives, everyone being the best that they can be and doing the best that they can do based on all that they know in this moment.

That is the beauty of the universe, of our life. We are always being and doing our best.

Once you truly understand and accept this truth, then life transforms. The need to judge others disappears. Once you really know that everyone is being and doing the best that they can, then what is there to judge?

When we are accepting and nonjudgemental, then we are completely grateful for what is, because we are accepting what is without the need to change it.

All acceptance and nonjudgement begins with you, with you being accepting and nonjudgemental of you.

Accept yourself as you are. You are the best version of you. When you know more, then there will be a new best version of you for you to accept.

Acceptance: simple, not always easy, but always worthwhile.

With love

x

325

*A*re you following your passion? How does it feel when you are following your passion? Do you know what your passion is?

Your passion is whatever lights you up, whatever you love to do. Something you'll always have time, energy and love for. What is it for you?

Your passion is not something you'll find by searching for it; your passion emerges so long as you are willing to continue to try new things and explore new opportunities with curiosity and commitment. Your passion emerges from your heart.

For your passion to emerge, your heart must be open and you need to be listening to what your heart is communicating with you.

Because our passion emerges from the wisdom of our heart, as soon as we follow our passion, we are in alignment with our heart and that is when the magic happens!

You deserve to connect with your heart and to follow your passion. You deserve it, and the world deserves to have you following your passion and truly living your life.

With love

x

326

*T*he creativity and inventiveness of humans is incredible. Things that seemed like science fiction only 20 years ago are now part of our daily life. Our creativity is a joy to behold!

For many people the amazing brilliance of technology has taken on a new role. Instead of being a set of tools we can use to simplify and enhance our lives, technology has become the source of distraction and diversion from what we really need to face in our lives.

Yes, we can communicate across the globe with a device that fits in our pocket. But how many of us need to have checked out social media at the start of the day and, depending on what we find on social media, the mood for our day is set?

How many of us are constantly keeping on top of our emails and messages, as if some terrible fate would befall us were a message to go unattended-to for more than twenty minutes?

Technology offers an abundance of opportunities to enhance our human existence. It also provides an abundance of opportunities to distract us from the challenges and opportunities that we need to embrace for us.

Technology was created to serve us. Notice how you are using technology and ask yourself if it serves you. Listen to the answer from your heart.

With love

x

327

Many times we feel a reaction to a situation but we don't acknowledge or articulate our feelings. This behaviour teaches us that how we feel is not worth acknowledging or articulating. It teaches us to not listen to ourselves.

Whilst we continue to deny our own voice, we are living out of alignment, because the inner voice that we deny is the voice of our heart. Our heart thrives and best serves us when it is heard.

Our heart is the source of our inner truth. Failure to acknowledge our inner truth draws us towards a joyless life of misery.

Begin by acknowledging the feelings that come up for you. Accept those feelings as what they are, a gift from your heart.

With love

x

328

*L*earn from your mistakes, is what we're told. And this is certainly better than beating yourself up.

But what if there was another way? What if there were no mistakes, only experiences? We would not be judging success or failure or mistake or not.

We could accept the outcome of our experience without judgement. Acceptance without judgement leads to a completely different life, a life of gratitude, love and abundance.

The shift from judgement to acceptance is transformative in your life and the life of those you interact with. Your energy will shift, causing you to radiate gratitude, love and abundance. Imagine how that feels for you and those you around you.

Experience life with acceptance and love.

With love

X

*B*est, grandest, kindest. How do you know when you are being the best you can be? Whether that's as a friend, a parent, at work, at home. How do you know?

What about the kindest or grandest or bravest? How do you know? What or who do you compare yourself with?

If you compare yourself with your perception of others, then you are setting yourself up for disappointment — disappointment with yourself, because your ego will always find someone who in some way is better.

How about if you knew that in every moment of every day, you are the best version of you that you could be based on everything that you know? How would that feel?

No more comparisons with others, no more opportunity for the ego to find someone or something better. Accept that today you are the best version of you that's ever been!

You are the best, the grandest, the kindest, the bravest you. Always.

With love

x

330

*T*his is the moment. The time is now. This is our time. We are likely to hear these expressions from time to time.

Notice how the word time is such an integral part of our daily language. It keeps us subconsciously focused on time, yet time is an illusion.

We invest much of our lives concerned with time. Not the present time but revisiting the past and anticipating the future.

There is a nothing wrong with planning for the future and recalling the past, but be sure to be present when doing the planning/recalling. By being present we are alive in the only time we truly have: this moment.

Allow yourself to be. To be present right here, right now.

With love

x

331

*T*he majority of humans lead a stuck existence, because most of us are stuck in our heads, therefore severely limiting the opportunities for our heart and soul to enable us to truly live instead of exist.

So often we might hear people ask where their head is on xyz or say that my head is telling me abc. Yet life is so much richer and more true when we notice how we are feeling and we give our heart the freedom to express and be heard.

The head was designed to be a tool of the heart, to carry out the activities that heads are good at, based on the direction and leadership of the heart.

Give your heart expression. Use your head based on the guidance of the heart and not the other way around.

With love

x

332

*W*e are all unique.

For some of us the idea of being unique, of being one of a kind is an idea that brings fear — the fear that we will stand out from the crowd, that we are different and that we might not fit in.

For some of us the idea of being unique is inspirational, energising, special. The fear for these people is to be lost as part of the crowd, that their uniqueness will not reveal itself.

The truth is that, like snowflakes, we are all unique, but we still belong to the same family, the family of humans. One of the beautiful aspects of humanity is the variety that is present in any gathering of unique beings.

Celebrate your uniqueness. Your uniqueness is essential to form the perfect gathering of humankind in which we exist.

With love

x

333

*W*hatever goes on around you, no matter how surprising, or upsetting, or disturbing remember to take care of you, take care of how you feel. Because through taking care of you, you are best able to contribute and serve those around you who are not able to take care of themselves right now.

Taking care of you begins with your heart and loving you, but not with protecting your heart or with keeping all your love for you. Quite the opposite.

Take care of your heart, so that you can open your heart to everyone around you, to share the love that's in your heart, to share it with gratitude and abundance.

If ever you find yourself in a situation where you feel unsettled and unsure of what to do, be love, be loving to you and to everyone around, simply love.

With love

x

334

Much of our human existence we are striving to achieve our goals, to meet a deadline, to get through to the weekend. We are moving (progressing?) at pace to cram everything into our human existence.

As we move seemingly faster and faster, to do more and more, we are completely missing the point. Life is only present in one place, and to experience life fully we need to be in that place. That place is now. It is this moment.

By slowing down, breathing deeply and noticing what's happening now, we experience life so much more deeply. We experience more of life when we are present.

It might seem counterintuitive but to experience more of life we do not need to move faster; we need to slow down, because then we are truly alive.

With love

x

335

*T*he love of our heart is unbounded and abundant. The love of our heart flourishes when being shared and interacting with the love from the hearts of others.

As humans, we are blessed with a heart, not simply the miraculous heart that beats at the centre (heart) of our physical body — as if that were not a blessing enough — but a heart that truly is our heart, a heart that, when we connect with it, manifests pure love.

Love is not a scarce, limited resource. Our heart has an abundance of love to share. There is more than enough for us and for everyone else, literally everyone else.

What's more, the world we live in feels completely different when love is the predominant emotion and feeling around us. When we are sending love to others, we are first and foremost sending love to ourselves. What a beautiful gift to us!

Connect with your heart and enable love to flow freely through you and beyond you.

With love

x

Tim Brister

*H*ow much do you love what you do on a daily basis? As you leap out of bed in the morning, how passionate are you about your life?

For many, many people, loving what they do and leaping out of bed are alien concepts not experienced since childhood, except perhaps at the weekend or on vacation!

Yet it is entirely our choice as to how we feel about our life, about each day, about each moment. And that choice is much less about what we do and much more about what we are being.

For example, when we are being love, truly being love, then our life experience in every moment is based on love. When we are being love we are also being grateful because love is always grateful. When we are being love we are also being compassionate because love is always compassionate.

Being love acts as a catalyst for so many other beautiful, loving ways of being.

Be love.

With love

x

337

*T*he world is a magical place. All around us, in every moment there is magic and miracles. Not everyone experiences the world in this way, but the truth is that magic and miracles are all around us.

Sometimes we don't notice the magic and miracles because we're so caught up in the current life drama that we've attracted to us. But the magic and miracles keep on coming anyway.

Once we understand and truly live each moment knowing that everything is a gift, then our experience transforms into one where magic and miracles are abundant. Of course, the abundant magic and miracles were always there; we just didn't acknowledge the gift in every moment.

Welcome magic and miracles into your awareness.

With love

x

*D*aily habits. What is it that you habitually do on a daily basis? How consciously have you chosen your daily habits? How well do they serve you to fulfil your dreams?

As uninspiring as it may sound, our daily habits determine the quality of our life. Who we decide to be and what we decide to do every day are fundamental.

Ask anyone who is living the life of their dreams and their lives will either have transformed in a single moment or they will have made a decision to transform their lives in a single moment. But what carried them to the life of their dreams and sustains the life of their dreams are their daily habits.

Champion sports performers achieve and maintain champion status through their daily habits. Those people with vibrant, healthy lives achieve and maintain that through daily habits. Beautiful, fresh, loving relationships are achieved and maintained through daily habits.

Choose your daily habits wisely. The quality of your life depends on it.

With love

x

*E*very challenge presents a fresh opportunity to become more of who you are and to enhance the world of those around you. How do you feel when you sense a challenge? Maybe your stomach churns, or perhaps your heart skips a beat.

The question is, what does that feeling mean to you? Do you interpret that feeling as one of excitement/anticipation of the challenge and the growth it will bring, or do you interpret it as one of fear of the challenge and likely change ahead?

That interpretation is going to determine so much about the quality of your life. Be sure to choose what is right for you.

You decide whether challenge promotes feelings of excitement or fear in you.

With love

x

340

*H*ow does your heart communicate with you? How much attention do you pay to the communication from your heart? Do you know when your heart is communicating with you? Or does everything your body acts upon come from your mind without the benefit of the wisdom of your heart?

One of the many miracles of human life is the resilience of all aspects of our mind, body and soul. Our heart will forever continue to communicate its wisdom to us; the only question is when we decide to pay attention to our heart.

The truth is that our mind is full of fear, and as with many humans, fear results in action; but because the action is borne out of fear, that action does not serve our greater good.

What the mind wants and needs is the wisdom of the heart. The wisdom of the heart is intended to guide the mind's incredible thinking power. This is the way we are designed to function for our greater good.

Listen to your heart. The wisdom of your heart will set you free in ways that your mind cannot even conceive. But, the heart also needs the mind, because what the mind does is use its power to support the desires and dreams of the heart.

Liberate yourself, listen to your heart.

With love

x

341

Many people feel some level of dissatisfaction with their lives, and they want to make major changes in their life. We hear claims of transformational change, and for many people transformation seems like a mountain that is not to be attempted, let alone achieved.

There are those that believe that transformational change is possible but that it's not sustainable. There are those who dismiss transformational change as impossible, believing that we are born as we are and so we will continue to be for this lifetime.

The truth is that transformational change is available for everyone and that it compromises a simple three-step process.

Firstly, vividly dream and envision your transformed life.

Secondly, commit to doing whatever it takes to be living that life.

Thirdly, take daily action consistently, action that supports your transformed life. Take small steps every day.

These three simple steps will enable you to move to your transformed life. These steps might be simple but they will not always be easy. They are certainly worthwhile.

Keep taking daily action for the life of your dreams. Your transformed life is yours to claim.

With love

x

Tim Brister

342

*T*he way in which we nurture the relationships in our life has a huge impact on the quality of our life. How much attention do you devote to nurturing your relationships?

One of the foundational aspects of human life is relationships.

Most people would view their relationships as being of different types. There might be intimate relationships, work relationships, friends, family, casual relationships, etc. However you describe the various relationships in your life, they are all relationships that flourish when nurtured.

There's one common thread running through your relationships, and that's you! And in order for your relationships to thrive, the primary relationship to attend to is the one that you have with yourself.

How do you treat you? How accepting are you of you? Is your love for you unconditional? Would you treat others in the same way that you treat you?

Take some moments to feel your truth, feel the answers to those questions, because you deserve to be loving to you. You deserve it for you, but you deserve it also for the deep love that enables you to share with others.

There's an expression that "the secret to living is giving". The place to start giving is with you. Start with unconditional love

for you and open the floodgates for unconditional love to flow through you and through your life.

Love you.

With love

x

343

*T*o acknowledge the beauty of your life and the perfection of your being is a divine acceptance of you. Acceptance of you and acceptance of what is are both essential to enable you to truly love you.

Many of us believe that our life is far from beautiful despite all the miracles and gifts that abound every single day. Accepting the beautiful miracle of life demonstrates a level of connection with the universe.

In contrast, the refusal to accept the beautiful miracle of life is acknowledgement of some disconnection, some misalignment with the universe.

When we are out of alignment with the universe, our life feels like a struggle. The universal energy is everywhere, so when we are not aligned with the energy of the universe we are setting ourselves up for a struggle with the universe!

Allow yourself to believe that life is a beautiful miracle. This belief will change forever your life experience. You will notice miracles, enjoy adventures, and live with love, including love for you.

Though you might find it hard to believe right now, by believing that life is a beautiful miracle you set yourself on a path to knowing that your being is indeed perfection. You have to trust that to be true.

Love the beautiful miracle of life.

With love

x

344

*A*lways expect the unexpected. Or to put it another way, let go of any expectations of the future.

Expectations are our prediction of how we believe the future will look. Yet we only ever live in the present; we cannot exist in either the past or the future.

Expectations are meaningless. They are our ego's way of keeping us out of the present whilst "designing" a future that we will never experience because we only ever live in the present!

Letting go of expectations, letting go of our desire to imagine our future sets us free from the treadmill of: create an expectation, never live in line with that expectation, get disappointed, long for a better future, set that expectation, get disappointed, etc., etc.

The treadmill of disappointment is a tool of the ego because it's a distraction that keeps you out of the present. It offers the illusion of a bright future that never arrives. But its most serious consequence is that it keeps you out of the present.

Any time you're out of the present is time in your life that you're not living and that you will never live. Every moment when you are not present is a moment that you've not been alive.

Live. Be alive. Drop expectations and live in this moment.

With love

x

Tim Brister

345

*H*ow do you choose to show up in every moment? Do you know that how you show up is completely your choice?

How we show up is such a huge factor in terms of how we experience our life. If you live every moment being grateful, do you think that your life experience might be different to you living every moment being judgemental or being love or being vengeful?

The magnificent choice that we have as humans is the choice about how we decide to be in every moment. That choice is a gift to be enjoyed and celebrated, but first and foremost it is a choice to be made.

We already make the choice how to show up; the question is how consciously we make that choice.

Choose consciously how you're going to be showing up in every moment. Let your heart choose, and enjoy your life experience based on the wisdom and love of your heart.

With love

x

346

*H*ow do you feel about your life? Is your life an adventure to be enjoyed, or a trial to be endured, or a battle to be fought, or a gift to be appreciated? Or something else?

Do you feel like life is happening to you, or that life is happening for you?

The truth is that your life is whatever you choose it to be. And whatever you choose, your life will manifest in that way. The universe understands your choice and always delivers!

Once you know that your choice is a free choice and that whatever you choose will be with you, then why would you choose to struggle or endure or survive your life? How about choosing to relish or appreciate or love your life?

Just for a day, choose to believe that every moment of your life is a gift. Try it for a day and notice how that day feels to you.

If that day of living life as a gift feels like the kind of day you'd like to feel again, then continue to live life as a gift.

Live life in a way that keeps you alive, loving and grateful. It's a gift.

With love

x

347

 Make today a day of love and compassion, where love and compassion flow through you and to those all around you.

Whatever the levels of love and compassion in your life, today be love and compassion even more than usual.

The day will consist of so many beautiful experiences for you and for those around you. And you'll never know the full implications and consequences of your love and compassion.

Because we live in a time where connections across the world happen in moments, one thing is for sure, the ripple effects of your love and your compassion will be felt quite literally around the globe.

An act of compassion can lead to another and yet another. There are many examples where an act of compassion has led to beautiful consequences way beyond that initial act.

But this is not all about creating a chain event of love and compassion. This is about you being love and compassion at a level you don't usually reach, just for a day. The growth, love and compassion that you experience will feel beautiful.

With love

x

*F*eeling the wisdom of the heart enables us to really connect with our true self. How well connected do you feel? How does the wisdom of your heart show up in your life?

Those occasions when you feel like you're in the flow, when it feels like everything you attempt is not only possible but it's an absolute joy — these are when you are connected to your true self, when your love and passion shines through.

Let go of the limiting, limited thoughts of the ego. The ego knows that once we enter that place of flow then we are truly connected with our heart, and this is when the ego knows that its control of us has gone.

Notice when you're in flow, when life is a breeze, when what you're doing is coming easy to you. Notice how that feels. That flow is always there for you, once you are connected with the passion of your heart.

Let go of limitations, open your heart, and flow.

With love

x

349

Life is unfolding perfectly in divine order for all of us in every moment of every day. For many people that statement will be met with resistance. But that resistance is an indication that they are resisting the perfect unfolding of life in divine order!

There are occasions when our life experience might feel at odds with the perfect unfolding of life. But that doesn't mean life is unfolding imperfectly; it means that we simply have not yet seen the gift in this moment.

Sometimes the gift of a moment manifests in our awareness in another moment. Let go of the desire for instant gratification and allow the beauty of life to unfold and be grateful for each and every moment. Then you'll much more readily feel the divine perfection of life unfolding.

With love

x

350

*T*he multitude of magical consequences that stem from being present, from living in the moment are gifts available to all of us in every moment.

This is because when we are present we are truly connected to ourselves and everything that is within our true self. Our creativity blossoms, our energy explodes, love is everywhere; we are present for others (what an amazing gift for them!), we are grateful, we are compassionate, etc.

Listen to your heart. Allow yourself the gift of being present, and watch as the true you reemerges. It's a truly beautiful gift to you and to the world.

With love

x

351

*E*ven when it feels like it isn't, everything is working out perfectly. The "catch" is that the perfection of life can only be experienced when we are present in this moment.

Whatever is happening in your life, however imperfect it might feel, ask yourself whether you are fully present. Are you fully present and therefore accepting what is?

In the present moment there is no resistance; there is connection, there is love, there is gratitude and there is acceptance. Once we accept what is, then we know that it's perfect as it is, right here and right now in this moment.

Be present, accept what is, love the perfection of life in this moment.

With love

x

352

Many of us are brought up to think of others before ourselves, to do more for others than we would do for ourselves. These principles come from a kind, loving place.

What is often overlooked is that in order to contribute beyond ourselves wholeheartedly and unconditionally, we must first nurture and love ourselves.

Once we love ourselves unconditionally we no longer subject ourselves to the destructive self-talk of our ego. We are free from the shackles of our ego, free to love others unconditionally.

Unconditional love flows freely; there simply are no conditions. We love without any expectation of what we will get in return for our love. We love simply because we know that we are love and that love is all there is.

Loving yourself unconditionally is a gift — a gift to you and a gift to the universe.

Enjoy the gift of unconditional love.

With love

x

353

*W*hat kind of energy do you feel in you? What kind of energy do you feel in those around you at home, with friends, at work, etc.? How much attention do you pay to the energy in your life?

Each one of us has an energy. When we enter any environment one of the first things that others will notice is our energy. They'll be (probably subconsciously) asking themselves what our energy is and how the energy of the environment has changed following our arrival.

Today, consciously notice the energy in your life. Notice how your energy ebbs and flows; notice any triggers that lead to your energy shifting.

Noticing your energy is the first step towards managing your energy. By noticing what triggers a change in your energy you get to choose whether your response to the triggers is serving you. Or perhaps a different response would serve you better?

Feel the energy in you and around you.

With love

x

354

Looking around, what do you see? Perhaps a world that's harsh, not always fair, perhaps a world where opportunities are limited to the lucky few. Or perhaps you see a world of limitless possibilities where miracles occur in every moment, a world where we can all choose our own path. Or perhaps something else?

The way in which you view the world has a huge impact on every experience in your life.

How did you decide on your worldview?

The truth is that few of us consciously determine our worldview. Most of us inherit our worldview from our family, peers, friends, teachers. We accumulate input as we go through our life and this forms our view of the world!

Perhaps now is the time to take a few moments to (re) construct your own personal worldview, to leave behind the inherited inputs that previously formed your worldview and to create a world as you would like it to be.

Our worldview really is a free choice, if only we'd realise it and make our own choice. It really will change your world!

With love

x

*W*e never really know what is going on for anyone else, what is happening in their life, what are their greatest dreams, their darkest fears. We never know what is in the mind of another, what chatter is going on inside of their head.

It's easy to look at others and to judge their behaviour. But what are we really doing? We are observing their behaviour through our eyes, through our life experience, through our current awareness.

We know that we can never know what is really going on for anyone else, so what is it we're observing? Our observation is coming from us; it is ours and therefore we can only be observing something that we know, some aspect of ourselves...

Consider that. We observe in others some aspect of ourselves.

Maybe there's a gift for us as we observe others as our awareness is brought to an aspect of ourselves that is crying out for our attention. Just maybe there's a gift there for us.

Celebrate the abundant gifts of the universe.

With love

x

356

*T*o what extent do you plan and schedule your life? Do you have goals you are working towards? How does the reality of your life experience match your schedule?

These are all good questions to consider from time to time. The really important related question is:

How do you decide to be as your life unfolds?

Because life experiences and events come and go, how you choose to be in every moment is up to you.

How about deciding that whatever happens is the perfect happening in that moment? It might not be aligned with your view of your life plan, but it is perfect.

However, if you accept every moment as a gift and recognise that there is a gift in every moment, then your reaction to life experiences and events will be very different and much kinder to you than if you believe that an event is not in line with your plan for your life.

Accept the gift of every moment.

With love

x

357

*E*ach and every moment of every day, our lives comprise an abundance of stimuli. We have many choices in each moment that affect our experience in that moment.

What do we choose to be? What do we choose to focus on? What meaning do we attach to that which we focus on? etc., etc.

From time to time we've all probably found ourselves in circumstances that we feel uneasy in. For example, we might be with others whose behaviour offends our values or beliefs.

We could choose to accept the circumstances as they are, or we could respond in a confrontational way in an attempt to change the behaviour of others, or we could choose to tolerate the offensive behaviour. Or we could choose something else.

The truth for us is that any response other than acceptance leads to some form of suffering for us. Being confrontational is based on our desire to change others; it's based on the false belief that our feelings are not fully our responsibility. This is not true; our feelings are 100% our responsibility!

Being tolerant means that we are suffering and putting up with their behaviour, which means that we are not taking full responsibility for our feelings.

With Love

Accept this moment as it is, because it is as it is. End your suffering.

With love

x

358

*T*here is a wide acceptance of mediocrity in our world today. This acceptance of mediocrity does not serve any of us.

The beauty for each of us is that we create our own experience and none of us are forced to create a mediocre experience. It's our choice, so instead of mediocrity let's create an awesome, fun-filled experience of contribution and love!

Some might not believe that mediocrity is widespread, but here are some day-to-day examples:

When asked how you are feeling, how do you respond? *Ok, all right, can't complain, not bad, could be worse*, or maybe if you're on top form you respond by saying *good*! How about feeling *awesome, outstanding, great, terrific, perfect*?

When you look to the future, do you truly believe that the life of your dreams is a life you will live? Or do you settle for being comfortable, or not risking too much, or staying in your current peer group so you don't upset them? How about you drop the self-made shackles and decide that you deserve the life of your dreams?

We are living mediocre, unfulfilling lives because we choose to. Decide to be awesome, decide to live the life of your dreams (not the dumbed down version of your dreams).

With love

x

*E*verything we do, we do it for a reason that makes sense to us in that moment. That applies to everyone. Even though it's sometimes challenging to understand the reasons of others, everyone does everything for a reason that makes sense to them in that moment.

Our reasons are always our own, based on our interpretations of our life experiences. We have many choices in every moment that contribute towards our actions in that moment.

We can never know what contributes towards the actions of others. Most people don't know what contributes towards their own actions, let alone anyone else's!

What's more, when we recall some of our own previous actions, we might know why those actions made sense to us at the time, because in this present moment, those actions no longer make sense to us.

Accept that everyone is being and doing the best that they can in each and every moment, and that as we remember and experience more, then our best will be different to that which it was. This is our journey.

Everything makes sense to us in the moment.

With love

x

360

*H*ow nurturing of yourself are you? We often find it more comfortable to care and nurture others yet we all deserve to be nurtured by ourselves first and foremost.

We all know people who have given of themselves to others, yet they have not taken care of themselves, leading to a life situation which means they are no longer able to contribute to others.

It truly is a gift to the world when we nurture ourselves.

Nurturing ourselves is an expression of our love for ourselves; we are being loving to us. The more loving we are to us, the more loving we are able to be in all our life. The more loving we are to us, the more loving we are able to be with others.

Love is abundant, it flows in and through us. The more loving we are, the more loving we are.

There is no lifetime limit on love; you don't run out of love as your age increases. The only way you feel like there's less love is if you are less loving.

Start by loving you, and the love in your life will flow with abundance and freedom. Free flowing love is a joy to behold, for everyone.

With love

x

361

*E*very moment of every day is a chance for us to change our experience. We could be having a "bad day", we could be feeling alone, we could be on top of the world. We could be experiencing our life in any number of ways.

And in that moment we are choosing our way of being, we are choosing the meaning we attach to each event; and we are choosing how we feel about that meaning. In every moment we choose.

Being present in each moment changes our experience of that moment. We are totally connected with ourselves and with that moment.

A simple action such as taking a breath and focusing our attention on that breath will enable us to be more present. It will give us the space to enable us to experience the current event in the present moment, where life lives and where we are alive.

Every moment is a gift. Appreciate your moments.

With love

x

Tim Brister

362

The world is such a beautiful place. There is beauty to be found all around; all we have to be is open to receiving that beauty in our lives.

Sometimes as we move through life we make things bigger and more complex than they really are. When we were children we were able to find beauty and wonder in every moment. If you watch a child at play they are always fully present in that moment and experiencing the beauty of that moment.

There is beauty in a loving friendship, a friendship with no expectations, a relationship where love flows freely and the most common sound is the sound of laughter. As children we enjoyed many relationships like this.

How many of your relationships are totally based on unconditional love, relationships where laughter abounds?

The more of these relationships that there are in the world, the more love and laughter there is in the world. Simple!

Enjoy the simple joy of a loving relationship. Bring more love and laughter to the world.

With love

x

363

*H*ow often do you go out of your way to express heartfelt gratitude? How does it feel for you when you express and when you receive heartfelt gratitude?

Many of us are brought up to say please and thank you because it's good manners. There's a whole different experience when heartfelt gratitude is expressed. Heartfelt gratitude is a whole world away from good manners.

Gratitude that is felt in our heart is also felt in the hearts of those to whom we are expressing our gratitude. Our interaction is at the level of our heart, which is where magical experiences are felt.

Heartfelt gratitude raises our connection to the level of our heart, enjoy the connection of our hearts.

With love

x

364

*F*rom time to time many of us feel out of sorts. Nothing is specifically wrong, we're experiencing a normal kind of day. Yet somehow something is unsettled inside of us.

It's probably the butterfly effect. We know that when a butterfly flaps its wings in the Amazon Rainforest then the ecosystem throughout the world is changed. The impacts of the flapping wings are felt across the globe, yet who is aware of the flapping of the butterfly's wings?

It's similar when we feel out of sorts for no reason that we can identify. Somewhere, someone with whom we are connected is flapping their wings. They have experienced an event which has affected their balance and because we are connected with them then we feel something within us which is disturbing to us.

The truth is that we are all connected, however, we have stronger connections with some and when those people flap their wings then we feel it in us.

So, go easy on yourself, don't stress and struggle when you feel out of sorts because invariably it will become clear which of the butterflies in your life flapped its wings and therefore, why you felt as you did.

With love

x

365

*W*here does your attention dwell? When you enjoy an experience does your attention dwell on the gratitude for the presence of that experience or the absence and the missing of the experience you enjoyed?

When a close friend is going away do you think about how much you'll miss them or feel gratitude for the fact that you are part of each other's life experience?

Whatever we consistently focus on, we get more of.

When your attention is focused on missing your friend, that's focusing on the absence of your friend and you'll get more absence in your life.

Whereas when your attention is focused on the gratitude that you feel for the loving relationship with your close friend then you'll get more loving close relationships in your life.

Life really is that simple.

With love

x

About The Author

Tim owns a number of businesses that enable him to develop a portfolio of services and products that enable his clients to transform their lives. Tim's portfolio includes relationship coaching, business leadership coaching, career coaching, trouble shooting in Financial Services, creation of experiential workshops and writing. Tim is purpose driven and his vision is to change the world, his clients experience change at many levels. The strength of Tim's contribution to his clients is demonstrated by the fact that the vast majority of his business comes through referrals from existing clients.

For the past twenty years, Tim has increasingly immersed himself in his own personal development journey through exposure to world-leaders in their field. Tim's refusal to accept anything other than the best for him and his family means he has personal experience of the tensions a parent has managing their need to contribute to their family as well as develop their career and/or business. Tim has been mentored and has become a mentor to many. Above all else, Tim is committed to living his truth, whatever that takes. One of the things that sets Tim apart is that he consistently brings all of himself to every client interaction.

Tim, having developed a specific coaching offering, continues to enjoy an amazing consulting career and a spectacular family life, which means that he is perfectly positioned to recognize both the challenges and opportunities many career-centric parents face. Leveraging his own experience,

Tim provides clients with a unique perspective on parenting, his clients consistently report dramatic improvements in all aspects of their lives. Tim coaches business owners and in corporates, through application of the principles that have proved so successful in his own life. Tim's belief is that business is simply an aspect of life, based on key aspects such as relationships and managing the tension of multiple important areas of life.

Having created a volume of inspirational quotes, Tim feels that these words best sum up Tim's message for the world: "Our planet is overrun with and run by fearful people. Don't let their conditioned fear diminish your beauty, your love and your dreams. Your heart knows the truth, let your heart shape your life".

Tim is purpose driven. His purpose is to change the world through his writing, coaching and workshops. Through working with others who are purpose driven, through that love and energy he is enabling millions to live their dreams, to express their truth freely from a loving place and to return to love and joy. Tim's passion for his purpose is matched by his energy and commitment to serve millions. It's a giant purpose and one that Tim is determined and dedicated to fulfilling.

Let's keep in touch

I would be delighted to hear of any ways in which these words have served you. And, if you feel drawn to me and my work please visit my website where you'll find details of the workshops and coaching services I offer. Here are my contact details:

Email: timjbrister@gmail.com

Website: www.timbrister.co.uk

FaceBook Page: Tim Brister

GOWOR
INTERNATIONAL PUBLISHING

Lightning Source UK Ltd.
Milton Keynes UK
UKOW06f0028170316

270296UK00001B/1/P